**The Plays of Edward Bond**

The aim of this short, accessible book is to offer help and stimulation to readers and theatre-goers who want to know more about Edward Bond's recurrent concerns as a playwright. In attempting to counter much of the received critical opinion about Bond's work, Tony Coult sets out to show how Bond's attitudes to religion and superstition, nature and politics, the family and the individual are given brilliant theatrical form in the plays. There are, too, chapters on the plays in performance, dealing with language and stage-craft, and on the often stormy history of Bond's relationship with the British Theatre. This makes for a fresh and unusual approach to a playwright's work, and one particularly suited to the closely related, 'rational' theatre of Edward Bond.

The Plays of
# EDWARD BOND

A Study by
# TONY COULT

**A Methuen Theatrefile**
**Eyre Methuen · London**

I would like to acknowledge the special help I have received in writing this book from the following: Edward Bond, Elisabeth Bond, Carolyn Gorney, Malcolm Hay, James Hasler, Lois Lambert, Philip Roberts, Richard Scharine.

This book is dedicated to my parents.

**T.C.**

First published in Great Britain in 1977 by
Eyre Methuen Ltd, 11 New Fetter Lane, London EC4P 4EE
Second, revised, expanded and illustrated edition, 1979

Copyright © 1977, 1979 by Tony Coult

ISBN 0 413 46260 9

Printed in Great Britain by Expression Printers Ltd, London N1

# Contents

## List of illustrations

### Background

### Gods

### The World

### Society

### Intimates

### The Individual v Art

### Stagecraft

## Quotations

Where a quotation is made from a published source, it is numbered and
keyed to the bibliography at the end of the book. Where no source is given,
the quotations are from letters and statements sent to the author by Edward
Bond and are used with his permission.

   All quotations from Edward Bond and from his work appear within
"double quotation marks". Quotations from all other sources are within
'single quotation marks'.

# INTRODUCTION

This book is not intended to be any kind of final critical judgement on Edward Bond's plays. That would anyway be a fatuous aim in the case of a writer who is, one hopes, only half way through his creative life. It is, rather, a guide-book, like those town guides which give you the basic history, and then take you, in words, on a 'perambulation' around the area, pointing out landmarks and places of importance. Its aim is to clarify what has been seen for those vaguely familiar with the area, and to introduce newcomers to something well worth their time and trouble.

It has constantly surprised me that any basic guide to Bond's work should be necessary, but the fact is that nearly fifteen years after the first staging of his work, he is still the subject of critical puzzlement, boredom and rumour-mongering. Although I don't support the idea that a writer necessarily deteriorates as soon as he gets on to an 'O' level syllabus, this official indifference and occasional hostility may be a good thing, a sign of the energy and danger vital for a healthy and relevant theatre. Nevertheless, as each new Bond play is produced, so the same old cliches of Bond criticism are wheeled blinking into the sunlight, perhaps less vigorous than in their salad days of 1965 and 1968, but no less deluded. Like most good writers, Bond can look after himself, and he can inspire great loyalty and commitment in his supporters. Nevertheless, it must be galling to know that you only earn your living by courtesy of productions in other countries; and for a writer to have to fight his way through thick draperies of cynicism and condescension each time he puts on a play must sap his energy a little, no matter how determined and confident he may be. The repetition at approximately yearly intervals of the old charges of 'gloating over violence', and the newer ones of 'naive politics', help neither the writer nor the theatre in general.

This book is an attempt to win back, in some small way, some of the ground lost, to make a claim for Bond as a writer whose startling and original theatrical imagination and craft have developed as a direct result of the need to understand and examine the dangerous, heaving world we live in. I have had to remind myself over and over again, when it seemed that I was stating the obvious, that the critical climate has consistently stifled any enthusiastic and intelligent response to Bond. If I am wrong, and Bond is not all I crack him up to be, then at least it can be said that some attempt at balance was made. This book will, I hope, soon put itself out of business because if it has anywhere hit upon truths, they will soon seem self-evident. In the meantime, I have tried to see these plays not as perfect or imperfect artworks to be categorised in textbooks and theses as more or less 'great' or 'significant', but rather as, in Wesker's phrase, 'tools for living'.

The form of the middle chapters is rather unusual, and fraught with some danger. I chose not to make a conventional play-by-play analysis because it seemed important to make a claim for the things Bond is saying about Man and society by pulling these ideas out into the open for inspection. After all, if these ideas are wrongly conceived, then the theatrical brilliance and the haunting imagination of Bond's work become just idle diversions, because what he says and the way he says it, grow, as in all the best art, from a common root.

The organisation of Chapters Two to Six is based on the idea that an over-riding concern of Bond's work is with structures that are inappropriate, and often severely damaging to human needs. I have imagined a human being as surrounded by a set of spheres, each one representing a group of related ideas which affect the life of that person. The outermost sphere, Chapter Two – *Gods*, deals with Religion and Superstition in the plays, with Man's relationship with the supernatural. Moving inwards, Chapter Three – *The World*, is about Man's relationship with the natural world, and with Man as an animal species. Chapter Four – *Society*, deals mainly with politics. It is appropriate that this chapter should be at the heart of the book, because all these spheres ultimately have political repercussions, and it is one of Bond's special skills that he is able to anatomise in theatre terms, the political implications of any human activity. Chapter Five – *Intimates*, deals with family and sexual relationships; and, finally, Chapter Six – *The Individual*, deals with psychology, with Man's relationship with himself. This chapter goes on to introduce ideas, such as Art and Imagination, that the individual can deploy to humanise himself and his society.

The first danger of this approach is the temptation to see each sphere as somehow distinct from the others. Ideally, perhaps, each chapter should be drawn on to transparent celluloid sheets and superimposed one on top of each other. The resulting image would give a more accurate picture of the way the ideas relate to each other. The second danger is that, in filleting out ideas in this way, the impression may be given that these plays are cerebral tracts, rather than the exciting and moving pieces of theatre which they are in performance. No-one who wants to enjoy Bond's work should miss an opportunity to see his plays on stage, even though the infrequent productions are sometimes inadequate. Reading the script is definitely second best, and reading this book no substitute at all.

# 1:BACKGROUND

The fact that Edward Bond is probably this country's finest living theatre writer is, of itself, not all that important. What is important is the fact that, far from acknowledging even a small part of his talent, most critics and commentators have in the past relegated his work to a small pigeon-hole in the history of the Royal Court Theatre. At most, they might acknowledge talent, but despise his world-view or his politics and wish he weren't quite so violent. (The confusion between the man, and the events of his plays, is a critic's problem too.) Probably only John Arden of recent British playwrights can match Bond for attracting such silly, mystificatory and abusive criticism. No-one would claim that Bond is beyond criticism but few critics seem able to match the plays' stubborn commitment to humane values with an answering generosity. Sometimes, even technical criticism becomes oddly distorted and discoloured by these prejudices. Bond's continued presence in the theatre is due in part to his own strong sense of his professional identity, and also to the early championship of a small group of theatre workers at the Royal Court, notably George Devine, Keith Johnstone and, above all, Bill Gaskill.

The story of Bond's involvement with the theatre sheds a fascinating light on the position of writers in society, and it is his awareness of himself as part of a particular class and social structure, an awareness present even when he was a child, which gives his plays their very personal flavour. Bond's grandparents lived in the tiny village of Shippea Hill in the Fens near Ely in Cambridgeshire. There they worked the huge, flat fields for all their working lives. His parents too were farm labourers who were forced to move during the thirties to find work in London, first to Holloway, where Bond was born in 1934, and three years later, to Crouch End. In 1940, as the Blitz began, he was evacuated to Cornwall: "I knew that I was being sent away so that I would not be killed by bombs. Not unreasonably, I thought that the fact that my parents were staying behind meant that they *would* be killed." That traumatic break, shared by many city children of his generation, seemed to strengthen and consolidate an acute sensitivity to his surroundings. Evacuation made him, he says, "aware of all sorts of things that one wouldn't normally be – just the change from London to the country was so striking that it brought one up abruptly . . . Actually to see a field for the first time when you had no expectation of ever seeing anything like that – well it's a very startling experience. And it made me very aware of people." [10] That kind of awareness, the vivid and intense experience common in children, is one of the qualities that make Bond such a memorable writer. No other dramatist of his generation so potently unites a precise, learned craft with the purity of vision of a child. Many of the childhood memories that he talks about in interviews share this quality. In Cornwall, he was boarded out with a childless couple whom he soon realised wanted children of their own: "I would walk out to the balcony and say 'Goodnight, mother'. I thought I was cheating because I did not feel she was my mother, so I knew I was doing it for some strategic reason. And at night my sister and I would tell each other stories – each telling half the story. The stories were heroic; they made us happy." [19]

Bond's childhood memories of war suggest a growing critical faculty: "At first, war itself came through as something heroic . . . Hitler, for instance, he just behaved in a way which was inhuman, grotesque." Later, however, war was to become more tangible: "I remember walking along a road and seeing two aeroplanes hitting each other, and I was terribly excited about this; it was marvellous, these great toys going smash in the air, two little silver aeroplanes, miles off. And I remember running down this hot road towards them, and suddenly out of the aeroplanes, two men appeared . . . it stopped me dead in the road, and made me realise that in fact what one had been talking about was human beings . . ." [10]

After the Blitz, he returned to London for a short time, and then stayed with his grandparents in Shippea Hill, finally returning to London for the war's end. It was then that war became directly threatening, as he and his mates dodged V.1's in the streets. In 1946, he went to Crouch End Secondary Modern School, but the only joy he had from lessons there was in composition, "the only lesson where we were creative, and it was a revelation to me". However, there was one event at school which proved to be crucial for Bond. This was a school visit to the Bedford Theatre in Camden to see Donald Wolfit's *Macbeth*: "For the very first time in my life, I met somebody who was actually talking about my problems, about the life I'd been living, the political society around me . . . there was just this feeling of total recognition. I *knew* all these people, they were there in the street or in the newspapers . . . I got a feeling of resolution – that there were certain standards." [10] After the play, Bond was surprised "that other people had seen this play, so how was it that their lives could just go on in the same way?" [10]

Politically, Bond was early an undefined "anti-Conservative", and he remembers taunting, with some other kids, a woman in black canvassing for Churchill in 1945: "We knew the class structure was dangerous and vicious." [19] But politics was as much a matter of experience as of conviction: "The reason that I'm interested in politics is that I grew up in a political situation where everything was seen in terms of politics . . . You were always involved in questions of necessity. Politics was the way one experienced growing up." [14]

After dead-end jobs in factories and offices, Bond was called up in 1953, and sent to Austria as part of the Allied Army of Occupation to work as a clerk. He found the army "one of the most outrageous institutions I'd ever encountered [4] . . . It was the nearest thing I've been to prison. Then I got a niche for myself and I really quite enjoyed it." [7] The army did not shake off that child's sense of justice: "You find in the army that the class structures are not glossed over . . . There was one thing I found disturbing – the military policeman swaggering and sauntering alone and a soldier in front of him marching. It was like a dog being trained. I've never forgiven him for that." [19]

It was probably the army with its peculiarly English mixture of sentimentality, brutality and routine, that finally politicised Bond. His soldiering experiences surface in *Early Morning, Narrow Road to the Deep North, Lear* and the opera libretto *We Come to the River*, and they are there, too, in *Saved*. While stationed in Vienna, he wrote his first 'serious' work, a short story. He began writing "to solve a puzzle, to find out exactly what it's like". [10] Soon after leaving the army, he began to write plays.

The man who set out, at 20, to write a play was, then, a half-educated labourer and clerk from a working-class family which had known a good deal of disruption, upheaval and poverty. The experiences of evacuation and National Service, and his knack for retaining into adult life his childhood sense of justice began to link up with a conscious awareness of class to create an intelligence which was both compassionate and critical. On top of that, he had an active imagination, and turned to words to express it: "I remember having some shoes bought for me and looking at the saleswoman while she tried them on for me. I noted the lines on her face and everything about her so that I would be able to describe her afterwards if I wanted to." In a curious pre-echo of his later encounters with the Lord Chamberlain, he once used the word 'prostitute' in a school essay, and got into trouble with his teacher. "I was surprised", he says, "because I had taken trouble not to use 'tart' – the word that came naturally. 'Prostitute' seemed to me a very proper, technical kind of word." The flair for words and the critical intelligence found plays the most natural medium: "I think partly it was towards the end of the fifties, and there was a great feeling about the theatre, and also partly because of the experience of *Macbeth*, so that one's mind naturally thought in terms of confrontations and speeches." [10]

Apart from *Macbeth*, and the awareness after 1956 that exciting things were happening at the Royal Court Theatre under George Devine, Bond's biggest cultural influence was popular variety. One of his sisters had at one time worked in a music-hall, being sawed nightly in half. The intimate audience-performer relationship of the music-hall, and the place that variety shows held in working-class culture remain as strong influences in Bond's analysis of his own job as an artist: "I don't see the plays I write as being intellectual in the sense of being cut off from a popular expression. I grew up at a time when the theatre was still part of popular experience in the music-hall. When I saw my first main play, which was *Macbeth*, I saw it in terms of the music-hall."

By 1957, Bond was embarked upon a number of projects with the aim of educating himself in the craft of the theatre. He spent two years seeing nearly everything there was to see in London, including, he ruefully admits, plays produced by the Moral Re-armament Movement. Of all the plays he saw, he was most impressed by the Royal Court productions, and by Joan Littlewood's work at Stratford East, which would have included Shelagh Delaney's *A Taste of Honey*, and Brendan Behan's *The Hostage*. At the Court, he would have seen Ann Jellicoe's *The Sport of My Mad Mother*, and Arden's *Live Like Pigs*. Keith Johnstone, a director at the Royal Court, soon established himself as a major figure in the Royal Court Writer's Group, which was beginning to meet under George Devine's guidance. He was the person directly responsible for involving Bond in the Royal Court, having read, in his capacity as the theatre's script-reader, two plays submitted by Bond, *Klaxon in Atreus' Place* and *The Fiery Tree*. *Klaxon in Atreus' Place* Johnstone remembers as being 'pretty psychotic, which to me seemed a good thing. I remember saying that we weren't likely to do the play, but the writer's talent was obvious.' Bill Gaskill, then one of the Court's directors, remembers 'a generalised atmosphere, cold and haunting'. Johnstone invited Bond to the Writers' Group, now run by Gaskill, in 1958; Johnstone, Gaskill and the Writers' Group between them provided a uniquely challenging and encouraging context in which Bond's talents could grow. More recently, 'alternative theatre' groups like Portable Theatre in the early seventies have performed a similar nurturing service, but the Writers' Group had one great advantage over these – regular access to a theatre with a stage big enough to require playwrights to learn about the problems of large-scale staging. The Group's main aims under Gaskill were to give writers a direct experience of acting techniques, including basic work on Stanislavski and Brecht, and mask work with Devine and Johnstone. The fact that directors ran the Group, and not writers, appealed to Bond. "It made the members aware of the plastic, visual nature of theatre. Traditionally, dramatists have always worked in the theatre, and acted, and got their awareness in that way." The Group remained fully active for some two years, but as individual writers grew more confident, and occasionally, successful, so the need for the Group passed. But the sympathy between Bond and Johnstone did not, and Johnstone now employed him as a playreader. Although Johnstone's subsequent career has centred on teaching and comedy improvisation, he and Bond shared a great deal, including a preoccupation with the innocence of children and the corrupting influence of adult society.

During this period of self-education in theatre, Bond did a line-by-line analysis of Chekhov's *Three Sisters*. By 1962, he was very much part of the Royal Court's community of artists, as a Writers' Group member, as a playreader (the best they had ever had, according to Johnstone), and even, on one occasion, as actor in a Sunday-night production. Thus, for a vitally important period, Bond was able to breathe the atmosphere of what Ann Jellicoe calls 'the idea of Direct Theatre – a theatre of action and images rather than words'. By this time, he had written about fifteen plays, including three intended for television. Those that he submitted to theatres and TV companies were rejected until the plays he sent to the Court, and it was while he was with the Writers' Group that he wrote *The Pope's Wedding*.

Once again, it was Keith Johnstone who recognised the play's quality. Early plans for Peter Gill to direct *The Fiery Tree* had fallen through, and so *The Pope's Wedding* became the first of Bond's plays to be staged. It was directed by Johnstone as a Sunday-night 'production-without-decor' (a format for giving new plays and playwrights the experience of staging with little economic risk). Bond was involved throughout in production, as indeed he has been in every subsequent first performance of his plays. (In 1978, he directed the first performance of *The Woman*, at the National theatre, and now intends to direct the premières of all his new plays.) The enforced lack of sets was no great disadvantage, as both writer and director were wary of them. Indeed, the emphasis on human actions above all else came to be a Royal Court house style. The play was, in part, an attempt by Bond to humanise the metaphysical images of tramps then fashionable, and he was particularly impressed by a production of Ionesco's *The Killer*: "What I wanted to do was try and get inside the image and see what it was all about."[10]

The critical reception of *The Pope's Wedding* was generally favourable. Most intriguing of all, in view of his more recent judgements of Bond, was Bernard Levin's in the Daily Mail: 'Yet this bizarre and unclassifiable piece is an astonishing tour de force for a first play, and if it comes to that, would be an astonishing tour de force if it were a fifty-first . . . Mr Bond is an original. We shall hear more of him.'

On the basis of *The Pope's Wedding's* relative success, Devine commissioned a new play from Bond, and in 1964, the theatre received a play called *Saved*. Initially scheduled as another Sunday-night to be directed by Johnstone, it was one of the scripts read by Gaskill, who had taken over as Artistic Director on Devine's death. His response to it was immediate and positive: "There are very few times in one's life when one is sure that a play is very, very good. And I had not a moment's hesitation over *Saved*." He swapped N. F. Simpson's *The Cresta Run* with Johnstone, and began work on *Saved*.

In June 1965, the script was sent to the Lord Chamberlain for licensing. The Royal Court had already had brushes with the Chamberlain's censorship functions, but what happened over *Saved* exceeded any previous dispute. It was returned with selected 'Buggers' and 'Christs' and the like removed, but also with the whole of Scenes Six and Nine cut. In addition, there were stern footnotes to the stage directions: 'The couple must not lie down on the couch so that one is on top of the other,' and, 'Pam must *not* undo Len's belt.'

After a fruitless visit to the Lord Chamberlain's office, which Bond was asked to stay away from in case he became undiplomatically angry, Gaskill decided to sidestep the censorship by presenting the play as a club performance for the English Stage Society. So, on 3 November 1965 *Saved* opened, and the storm broke.

It would be cheap and easy to jibe again at the critics who were genuinely shocked by the play, but the press reaction was so virulent (with honourable exceptions) that it raised the issue of censorship by critical hostility just as forcefully as the struggles with the Lord Chamberlain had raised the issue of censorship by the State. Edward Bond has certainly wasted useful time writing filmscripts to earn a living because his plays have a dour reputation owing in great part to a tiny handful of critics. Bond himself fought back over *Saved* with letters to the press: "It is an extraordinary comment on the state of our theatre, our theatre critics, and perhaps our morals, that any reasonable critic could think that a serious dramatist would write a scene as horrifying as the murder scene in *Saved* in order to provide 'an opportunity for vicarious beastliness . . . the new English drama will not fulfil its promise unless a) censorship goes, and b) criticism becomes more informed, competent and objective."

The Royal Court responded to the uproar with a public discussion chaired by Kenneth Tynan, at which sympathisers such as Mary McCarthy and Ronald Bryden, and hostile critics such as J. W. Lambert and Irving Wardle confronted Gaskill and Bond. Meanwhile, one of the play's most dedicated patrons was a Chief Inspector Rees of the Flying Squad, who saw the play no fewer than five times. On his evidence, and that of other playgoing police officers, the theatre was prosecuted the following February for presenting *Saved* without a licence, club status notwithstanding. Ironically, as the hostile publicity grew, business, which was poor to begin with, picked up considerably towards the end of the run. Nevertheless, on April Fool's day 1966, the Marylebone magistrate found the defendants guilty, conditionally discharged them, and ordered them to pay £50 costs. Bond was, personally, very shocked by the uproar and the prosecution. Before the play opened, he had told an interviewer that he thought audiences would be "sympathetic to almost everyone in the play". [1] Afterwards, he said, he felt as if he had been kicked to death.

In January 1966, before the court case had taken place, Gaskill directed Middleton's *A Chaste Maid in Cheapside* with minor emendations, and a new ending, by Bond, who was also beginning work with Antonioni on the screenplay of the film *Blow Up*. At this time too, *Saved* was being sought after in many European countries. This pattern – Bond being sustained by foreign productions and film-scripting – continued until about 1969-70. He now disowns all his film-work, and once described the general style of *Nicholas and Alexandra*, to which he contributed, as "sentimental vulgarity". An exception could perhaps be made for Nicolas Roeg's *Walkabout*, which despite its occasionally over-ripe desert photography, has the merit of preserving at least some of Bond's script and themes. More interesting at a time when a court case was hanging over his head, was the Arts Council bursary of £1,000 (offered *before Saved* was performed) which enabled him to continue work on a project conceived before *Saved*, a comedy about Siamese twins.


In 1967, Gaskill decided to direct *Three Sisters*, and it was therefore natural that he should ask Bond, who had carefully analysed the play, to provide a translation. The production attracted most attention for the casting of Marianne Faithfull as Irina, and Bond's translation was not much remarked upon, a point, one supposes, in its favour. By now the 'comedy about Siamese twins', commissioned by Gaskill in 1965, had formed itself into *Early Morning*, and it was presented to the Lord Chamberlain. This time it was banned outright, without explanation, although it obviously did contravene the protocol on stage presentations of the Royal Family. The decision was made once again to present the play as a club performance, with everyone hoping that the pressure to abolish censorship would oblige the censor to leave the theatre unmolested. It did not. The Lord Chamberlain indicated in advance that the play would be prosecuted, and so it was decided to mount it for two club performances before invited audiences at the Royal Court on 31 March and 6 April. In the event, the theatre's licensee, Alfred Esdaile, evidently intimidated by police enquiries after the first performance, unilaterally cancelled the second evening. Gaskill therefore arranged an afternoon open rehearsal for critics to see. Esdaile responded by offering his resignation, demanding Gaskill's suspension, and delivering himself of this verdict: 'The play has no artistic merit and I think Mr Gaskill and Mr Bond are doing it just for the publicity.'

*Early Morning* thus became, even more than *Saved*, a confusion of political and aesthetic issues, and of the few critics who saw it or read it, fewer still seemed to approve of it. After the apparent naturalism of *Saved*, this breath-taking and haunting play, into which Bond had put so much energy and personal commitment, was too much to take. In the face of this general puzzlement, and particularly that of Irving Wardle in The Times, John Arden came to Bond's defence in a letter to the paper: 'I have myself had one play, widely described as "muddled and untalented" performed on a Sunday at the Court. This production was of enormous value to my subsequent career as a playwright. It seems a pity that Mr Wardle could not have added to his legitimate criticisms of *Early Morning* a note of joy that he was enabled to see the play at all.' As if anticipating his problems, Bond had written a piece for the short-lived magazine The Critic in which he analysed the problems and limitations of critics. His conclusions were hardly going to endear him: "Critics have been forced on to the theatre by the peculiarities of modern social living, and the danger is that they will damage the theatre by clinging to their old informed cultured, civilised, balanced standards. These standards, and the whole culture that gave them meaning, died about forty years ago." [23]

In May of 1968, Bond won the George Devine Award for *Saved* and *Early Morning*, and he spent 2½ days, bought by his film-writing, pulling together *Narrow Road to the Deep North*. The play, sharing many themes with *Early Morning*, had been germinating in note form for some time, but the speed with which the final script came together is still remarkable. The commission to write it came from Canon Verney of Coventry Cathedral, chairman of the 'Peoples and Cities Conference' held in the city in 1968. Three or four writers were asked to write a piece for the occasion, but Bond, who was not the Conference's first choice, was the first to accept. It was undoubtedly a courageous move on Canon Verney's part given Bond's newly-acquired reputation. The Coventry Standard alluded to '32-year-old Edward Bond, hottest product in Britain's "shock 'em rigid" playwriting belt', and there was yet another brush, albeit minor, with the Lord Chamberlain, requiring Canon Verney to travel to St. James's Palace to intercede on the play's behalf. Bond wanted Gaskill to direct the play, but Gaskill had not taken to it, and so offered it instead to his assistant Jane Howell, who had acted Joyce in *Early Morning*, and assisted him on *Saved*. She has since become closely associated with the play, describing it as 'the most important work in my own develop-ment'. Backed by a £500 grant from ATV, the play opened for its short run at the Belgrade Theatre on 24 June 1968. The local press, having worked themselves into a lather about it, seemed mildly disappointed that the play was not the outrage they had been expecting. Nationally, the play was liked because, most critics felt, the 'nasty bits' had been contained in a distancing, neo-Brechtian framework. Some even suggested that Bond had resorted to allegory as a response to censorship, a view supported later by both Gaskill and Jane Howell. However, the apprentice work before *The Pope's Wedding* included allegorical plays, and the apparent shift in style between *Saved* and *Early Morning* has more to do with Bond's progress as a craftsman, and Bond's thinking about *Early Morning* had in fact started before *Saved*. *Narrow Road to the Deep North* went some way to demythologising Bond, but although it is a fine play, an unfortunate critical cliché has developed that claims it as his best, whereas *Early Morning,* a vastly more ambitious work and therefore easier to fault, is supposed to be immature and full of wild, undigested material.

During 1968, Bond received, jointly with Peter Barnes, the John Whiting award for *Narrow Road to the Deep North*, but it was the following year that marked a real turning-point in his career when the Royal Court, at Gaskill's instigation, mounted revivals of *Saved, Narrow Road to the Deep North* and *Early Morning*. This exceptional gesture of support for a writer was possible because the Theatres Bill had finally become law on 29 September of the previous year, and stage censorship was no more. *Early Morning* had been its final victim. As well as making a claim for Bond's stature as a theatre writer, the season of revivals allowed Gaskill and Jane Howell to rework their productions, and in the case of *Early Morning*, to give a first, full production. *Saved* acquired more sophisticated sets, and sequences of slides showing random advertisements, newspaper cuttings and comic-strips to cover scene-changes, while Jane Howell experienced intriguing problems adapting her production of *Narrow Road to the Deep North* from the wide stage at Coventry to the far narrower confines of the Royal Court. Both directors made the inevitable cast changes with added sureness. With few exceptions, all of them seem to have been improvements.

*Saved* had a third revival in 1969 in a short run prior to a tour of Eastern Europe by the Royal Court company, sponsored by the British Council. The tour, which also included *Narrow Road to the Deep North*, was to Poland, Czechoslovakia, Yugoslavia and Venice. *Saved* was received with respect but not much love, perhaps because the social details were removed from the cultures of those countries. The allegorical form of *Narrow Road to the Deep North* was far easier to understand, especially, it seems, in Czechoslovakia, where it arrived just one year after Russian tanks had occupied Prague. At the BITEF festival in Yugoslavia, the company won joint first prize, but despite that accolade, three years later a Parliamentary Expenditure Committee found it 'hard to believe that the plays of Edward Bond . . . would have been fully understood by theatregoers other than expatriates and a small intellectual élite'.

The first of a body of short plays written at the request of various political groups or fringe theatres appeared in 1970 with *Black Mass,* written for an entertainment at the Lyceum Theatre sponsored by the Anti-Apartheid movement to commemorate the Tenth Anniversary of the Sharpeville Massacre. Directed by David Jones of the Royal Shakespeare Company, this surreal little satire was one of a number of plays and events written for the evening. The casting coup was probably the silent part of Jesus Christ, who descends from the cross to poison the South African premier's communion

A play for a rock concert – *Passion* at the C.N.D. Festival of Life 1971. (Photo: Tony Coult)

A play for the National Theatre – *The Woman*, Olivier Theatre 1978. (Photo: Chris Davies)

wine. He was played by Edward Bond, "so that I could tell my grandchildren". In the same year, the Committee for Nuclear Disarmament asked Bond to write for the Easter Festival, but the notice was too short. He did, however, offer to write for the 1971 Festival, and the result was *Passion*, which also featured Christ. Its theme was determined in part because Bond knew that it was to be performed on Easter Sunday. Brighton Combination theatre company were initially to perform it, but they decided, with admirable integrity, that they could not then do it full justice. It passed to Unity Theatre, who in turn heard that the Royal Court were prepared unofficially to sponsor it, and so they too backed down. The director, Bill Bryden, was then Gaskill's assistant. (They had previously worked together on *Early Morning*.) The performance took place on the main grandstand of Alexandra Palace Racetrack, to an audience of some 3,000 people, a great many of whom sat in the grand-stand itself, with the actors using a Tannoy system to cope with the outdoor setting. Very little reviewed, the successful performance of *Passion* was a great tribute to the clarity of Bond's style, both in its language and its stagecraft.


The period 1969-71 seems to have been relatively a fallow one for Bond, partly perhaps because of the expenditure of energy in writing and fighting for *Early Morning,* his "freedom play". He was also writing film-scripts, and the idea for a new version of *Lear* was beginning to take shape. It was, originally, to be a variant of the three sisters theme, playing down Lear and emphasising his daughters, but that idea became subsumed in a radical reassessment of the King. During this period of work, Bond collaborated with director Keith Hack on translation and adaptations of Brecht's *Roundheads and Peakheads*, itself an adaptation of *Measure for Measure*, a play that fascinates Bond. The end results were not to his liking, but he had, in the process, taught himself about Brecht, as he had earlier taught himself about Chekhov.

*Lear* was to be performed by the Royal Court, but it was to open in September 1971 at the Belgrade Festival, where *Saved* had earlier won its prize. However, the British Council, clearly now disturbed by Government strictures, failed to provide the balance of the cost, which would have been largely borne by the Festival. It therefore opened on 29 September at the Royal Court to the kind of intense notices that had not been seen since *Saved*. 'Throughout this collage of sickness', wrote Judith Cook in the Birmingham Post, 'where facetiousness rubbed shoulders with Grand Guignol, I refused to see anything but a bad play.' On the other hand, Frank Marcus, himself a playwright, although of a very different kind from Bond, wrote in the Sunday Telegraph, 'It is astonishing and shameful that a work of this magnitude was not offered the facilities of the National Theatre.' Unfortunately, the overall impression given by the notices was of something cold, painful, faintly disgusting and finally boring. The houses became so poor that the theatre took an advertisement in the Sunday Times, inviting readers not to be misled by critics, but to see for themselves. It invoked both *Saved* and *Serjeant Musgrave's Dance*, as earlier victims of critical blindness. Before the end of the run, many German theatres alone had made enquiries about presenting the play, and negotiations were in hand with Czechoslovakia, France, Italy,

Sweden and Denmark. Gaskill's production was very successful considering the enormous technical problems of the large cast; also notable was the technical accomplishment by the designer, John Napier, in the fitting of Lear's wall on to the Court's open stage. *Lear* is remarkable because it summons up Shakespeare's play, yet exists entirely free of it as an autonomous work of art.

Bond's next play was *The Sea*, which opened at the Royal Court on 22 May 1973. Originally called *Two Storms*, this was a play that seemed mellower, and therefore 'safer'. Bond himself told an interviewer: "The balance is different this time in that I deliberately set out to make an audience laugh. When I wrote *Lear*, I wanted to say 'All right, I'm going to make demands on my audience'. In *The Sea*, I had a different intention. I wanted deliberately to say to an audience 'You mustn't despair. You mustn't be afraid'." [12] *The Sea*, comic and haunting, introduced a major difficulty for those to whom the dramatising of the tough social truths of *Saved*, with its almost total lack of rhetoric, was Bond's greatest talent. The problem was exemplified by Evens' final speech. In *Lear*, Bond gave the King a degree of symbolic language and rhetoric because the play showed a process of learning, and it was appropriate to Lear's situation that he should articulate that process to himself. Evens' articulation, what Bond calls the "celebration of articulacy" that ends the play, invites the criticism that Bond is abandoning a knack for showing ideas-in-action in favour of the simple manipulation of his characters into talking about their ideas. The trouble with this argument is that it ignores the fact that Bond is writing about articulation *as action*. It is a daring experiment of a particularly unfashionable kind for a writer like Bond to attempt, and perhaps it is not wholly successful.

*The Sea*, dedicated to and directed by Bill Gaskill, seemed at the time a godsend to more conservative critics and a possibly dangerous portent for his more impatient supporters. Neither seems an adequate position from which to describe this funny and idiosyncratic play.

*Bingo*, subtitled 'Scenes of Money and Death', likewise disappointed some admirers, and gave rise to the criticism that it was an introverted, literary work, concerned only with artists' private pains, because it was an extended speculation about the last years of Shakespeare's life. Certainly, for much of the play, the dispossessed poor who lived around Shakespeare form a background in front of which Shakespeare nurses his self-contempt. In the theatre, that balance seems justified because it reflects the world through Shakespeare's eyes. Certainly, Bond has written a very personal play, although not one which is anything like as limited as has been claimed. *Bingo* tests Shakespeare's life against Bond's own ideas about the artist's social role, but it is also about defining anybody's relationship with society, and the responsibilities each person bears for what goes on inside it. *Bingo* was written for Jane Howell, who directed it with John Dove as her departing show at the Northcott Theatre, Exeter, opening on 14 November 1973. Those critics who made it down to Exeter seemed to find it a deeply pessimistic work on a fascinating theme. Bond replied to Harold Hobson's criticism in The Sunday Times in a piece which denied that *Bingo* was pessimistic. Predictably, the play was taken much greater notice of when it transferred to the Royal Court with Sir John Gielgud as Shakespeare, and this production actually broke box office records at the theatre.

On 24 March 1974 a translation by Bond of Wedekind's *Spring Awakening*, a play which shares many of Bond's preoccupations about education and freedom, opened at the Old Vic mounted by the National Theatre. As W. Stephen Gilbert pointed out in Plays and Players: 'It is not hard to see Bondian devices, images and even characters in *Spring Awakening* – the burial of Moritz making a pair with the burial in *The Sea*; the fable which anticipates fate; the desperate violence, sudden like a death; the pellucid cameos of authority; the notion of 'moral insanity'; the wall as all-purpose image of repressive structure; the austerity of language; the unquiet dead.'

In 1975, one of Bond's sisters died from lung cancer and the experience of watching her illness and death affected him deeply, such that he wrote a play called *Palace of Varieties in the Sand,* straight off, with little preparation. He has, however, now withdrawn this play.

In between *Bingo* and his next major play *The Fool*, Bond worked on an adaptation of Ibsen's *The Master Builder*, which was never used, for the Los Angeles-based television company Community TV of Southern California.

The end of 1975 saw *The Fool*, subtitled 'Scenes of Bread and Love', about the Northamptonshire poet John Clare, his life and subsequent madness. Whereas *Bingo* was about the artist's responsibility to society, *The Fool* was about the artist's rights in society, and, just as in the earlier play, the artist's problems became exemplars of problems faced by all members of society. Bond explained that he wasn't interested in the story of Clare for its own sake: "I'm not asking for justice for Clare or anything like that. I'm only interested in it in that it's a paradigm for our own age, in the way it reflects on our own problems." The play was directed at the Royal Court by Peter Gill, Bill Gaskill having left to co-direct the Joint Stock Theatre Company.

While *The Fool* was running, a piece appeared in New Society, written by Albert Hunt, one of the few critics whose own work in theatre and education matches Bond's in innovation and humanity. Hunt conceded Bond's skill in creating dramatic images which make a sense of violence concrete and immediate, but felt that Bond 'has been trapped by his own literary aspirations and has lost touch with the society he was trying to explain . . . it's not so much a question any longer of a "writer's theatre", as a theatre about writers.' That analysis, attractive as it sounds to anyone who would give a dozen *Bingo*'s for another *Saved*, has to be recognised as essentially snobbish, and on Albert Hunt's part, self-deprecating. Its hidden assumption is that artistic work has, intrinsically, less value than other work, that the problems artists meet are somehow different in kind from, and less significant than, the problems facing anyone else. It also assumes, I think falsely, that only artists can enjoy plays about artists. Ironically, the commitment to the creative imagination as the key to any humane politics, which is what *The Fool* is all about, is exactly the same commitment that

Albert Hunt brings to his own work.

*Stone*, a short play written to commission for the Gay Sweatshop theatre company, may have confirmed the worst fears of those who disliked Bond's allegorical style. Gay Sweatshop, a group committed to homosexual liberation, had decided to commission non-gay writers in a move to broaden the base of their work. The play they received was a short parable closely related to Bond's short stories. The play opened at the ICA Theatre on 8 June 1976, and the fact that it nowhere mentions homosexuality seemed to cause confusion. John Lahr's comments in Plays and Players sum up the fears that were now being expressed: 'Bond's allegory indulges his appetite for philosophy, when his genius is in evoking the dynamics of personality and suffering in specific situations.' Michael Coveney, on the other hand, wrote in The Financial Times: 'This is not only one of the best lunchtime plays for months, it is also one of the best short plays I have ever seen.' *Stone* does indeed have remarkable qualities, and is, again, the result of a developing artist's willingness to court dangers and to overcome them.

As if to point up the great variety of working situations available to Bond, 1976 saw the premiere at the Royal Opera House, Covent Garden, of the opera *We Come to the River* by Hans Werner Henze, with a libretto by Bond closely related to *Lear*. Bond has an intense interest in music, including Henze's. A mutual friend introduced them, and their talks about collaboration initially revolved around a version of *Edward II* by Marlowe. Bond, however, wanted to attempt something original. The opera, with its vast instrumental and vocal forces and its teeming stage pictures, opened on 12 August. The presentation of this neo-Marxist opera in a costly production at Britain's premier opera house was a startling contradiction which cast a penetrating light on statements made by Bond and Henze on the need to write for the working class. Whatever the debate over form may be, it certainly demonstrated that the working-class are effectively denied ownership of any large-scale means of theatre production.

The end of the busy year of 1976 saw the fruition of another fringe-theatre commission. Ed Berman of Inter-Action had asked Bond to write for a season at the Almost Free Theatre to coincide with the American Bi-centennial of that year. He received a double-bill called *A-A-America!*, consisting of two plays, *Grandma Faust* and *The Swing*. (Bond was, in fact, the only writer in the season who could be said to have dealt directly with America.) Jack Emery's productions were plagued with misfortunes including injury to an actor, and a pay dispute, and the planned double-bill of the two plays occurred only twice. Out of these problems, however, *The Swing*, in which Bond was heavily involved directorially, emerged as one of his fiercest, most direct, most compassionate plays. *Grandma Faust*, a playfully cerebral companion piece about racism provided a nimble counterpoint to the darker world. But it is the awesome power of *The Swing*, the absolute certainty with which Bond handles the terrible events and the polemical energy that drives his craft, which all attest to the fact that Bond is far from slipping into a 'soft' mid-career. On the contrary, he is a continuing experimenter. Only an explorer, having written *Saved* would tackle *Lear*, or risk the accusation of literary infatuation by writing *Stone* or *Bingo*. Consider the range of his work: he has accepted commissions from groups like Gay Sweatshop and

Inter-Action, and he has written a play for performance outdoors before 3,000 people at what was, in effect, a rock concert. He has co-written an opera and, subsequently, a ballet, as well as a series of major plays for the Royal Court which have been performed in theatres all over the world. He writes poetry, short stories and polemic, and is involved in the political life of the theatre. He was, for instance, a founder member of the Theatre Writers' Union, which now includes most of the country's leading playwrights, and was responsible for an attempt to democratise the Royal Court's management during its 1977 crisis.

1978 saw the production of *The Bundle* at the RSC's Warehouse Theatre. It was directed by Howard Davies, a director particularly sympathetic to Bond's style who had specialised in Brecht and directed *Narrow Road to the Deep North* and *Early Morning* at the Bristol Old Vic, and *Bingo* for the RSC at the Other Place. This, to date Bond's latest play, is the first of a new series.

Later in 1978, Bond directed *The Woman* at the National Theatre. It had been gestating for some eight years, and was finished before *The Bundle.* The production needed a large-scale theatre space to encompass its epic proportions, and found an appropriate home on the stage of the Olivier Theatre.

In 1978, Bond took up a Northern Arts Literary Fellowship at Newcastle University. During that time, as well as taking workshops and seminars with students, he wrote *The Worlds*, which received its first performance at Newcastle Playhouse on March 8 1979. Directed by Bond, the play was acted by students of the University and Polytechnic at Newcastle. *The Worlds* is the first full-length, published play of Bond's to be set in the present since *Saved.* It is a play in the didactic tradition of Brecht's *Lehrstücke.* It sets out to discern the real truths and the political reasoning behind terrorism, in a plot based around the kidnapping of a business chief to support a strike against his firm.

The first London production of *The Worlds* took place on November 21st 1979 at the Royal Court Theatre Upstairs. Bond again directed the play, and his actors were again young people, members of the Royal Court Young People's Theatre Scheme.

Another Henze/Bond collaboration was staged in 1979 by the Stuttgart Ballet, called *Orpheus.* Composer and playwright are currently engaged in a new opera project.

1978 and 1979 were years, for Bond, of production, of teaching, and of reflection upon the craft of theatre. 1980 will be devoted far more to the writing of plays, including a new libretto for Henze and a musical comedy. There will, too, be a series of theoretical papers and some longer poems about theatre and politics.


The problems Bond has had, and still has, in finding acceptance as a writer of great quality may have to do with his ease of passage from one theatre form to another. Another obstacle to easy acceptance is that he dares to make large theatrical statements about the kind of complex issues which a basically philistine and fragmented culture such as ours finds it embarrassing or portentous to discuss.

What is Bond, then? A philosopher or a propagandist? A theatre technician or a literary artist? The truth is, of course, that he is a playwright, like Brecht, who combines all these skills. Like Brecht, he turns his hand to many different forms, and like Brecht, his writing can be complex to express the difficulty of an issue or simple to express its urgency.

When he started seriously to write for the theatre, Bond saw a span of plays that began with *The Pope's Wedding* and ended with *The Sea.* After that, he wrote three plays, *Bingo, The Fool,* and a new play *The Woman – Scenes of War and Freedom,* set in the Trojan Wars. These are historical plays, whose function is to demythologise eras which might tempt us to see them as 'golden'. That series of three plays is now over, and Bond has embarked upon a third phase of writing, beginning with a reworking of the Basho story, and entitled *The Bundle.* The distinguishing feature of this third series of plays seems to be a growing sense of confidence: "We mustn't write only problem plays, we must write answer plays – or at least plays which make answers clearer and more practical. When I wrote my first plays I was naturally conscious of the weight of the problem. Now I've become more conscious of the strength of human beings to provide answers. The answers aren't always light, easy or even straightforward, but the purpose – a socialist society – is clear."

The immediate future, with economic recession inevitably limiting the production of uncommercial large-scale work, may prove difficult, but Bond will certainly continue to write challenging and disturbing plays. There is no-one else working today with his combination of poetic imagination, sound theatrecraft, and an intense, generous confidence in people. As the poem chalked on the wall of the Almost Free Theatre during *The Swing* emphasised: "The future is pleasurable".

# 2:GODS

Edward Bond is an atheist and a humanist. These are facts basic to an understanding of what goes on in his plays. His work invariably embodies a tough
critique of the unholy alliance between religion and political power.
Sometimes religious belief is shown to be a poisonous soil from which grow
cruel and destructive weeds, and sometimes it is seen to be appropriated,
after the event, as a cloak to hide the real business of power. But Bond's
analysis searches deeper than the outward show of religious belief. In the
end, he attacks a frame of mind which hands over to gods (and even to men
who try to transform themselves into gods) responsibility for what happens to
human beings. His criticisms of religious thinking form the vanguard of an
assault upon all structures, political, social, and psychological, that confine
human freedom.

Bond's plays are, nevertheless, haunted by religious ideas, images and
characters, in much the same way that our irreligious and fragmented culture
is still haunted by the ghosts of its believing past. When he writes about
religion, it is often as superstition, as a specific fantasy generated by a culture
and consolidated in individual minds, whose function is to cope with material
fears and anxieties. Bond has talked about the strong influence some
Christian ideas and images had upon him as a child. He remembers walking
the streets of Crouch End in North London "terrified to think how God was
love, and he killed his son for us and hung him up and tortured him and
washed us in his blood".[4]  A theologian could perhaps explain that bloody
paradox but the young Bond could not, and it is reasonable to suppose that
most kids who encounter it cannot. That it remained with Bond as an
unacceptable face of religion is shown even in his first performed play *The
Pope's Wedding*. Here, Scopey, a young farm labourer, enters into a half-
caring, half-dominating relationship with an old tramp Alen. He forces Alen
to sing for him, and this bizarre hymn is the result: "Little babe nailed to the
tree/Wash our souls in thy pure blood/Cleanse each sin and let us be/
Baptized in the purple flood . . ." And so on, in a marvellous parody of
Christian hymnody, full of the legitimised violence that so offended Bond as a
child. "What one can have as a child is religious fear, and I think I had a
certain amount of this."[10]

Evacuation during the war made him, he says, "aware of all sorts of things
that one wouldn't normally be . . . In Cornwall, you got all these curious
religious sects – I remember marching over the hills in an enormous crocodile
of children, carrying this banner, struggling up the hills. God knows what it
said."[10] These vivid memories are, like fairy-tales, instinct with a sense of the
unknown and the fearful. What offended Bond, and does so still, is the fact
that these fairy-tales are still offered as truth.

Bond grew up in wartime, and knows what it is like to be bombed, so there were obviously violent threats enough to confirm at least the possibility of an event as dreadful as the Crucifixion. These must have been startling and impressive experiences, but it should not be assumed that they are unique to Edward Bond. Most infant and junior schools in the 1970's teach children about Jesus, and very many working-class children living in cities have undergone, in the name of redevelopment and planning, disruption and unhappiness not so different from that experienced by wartime evacuees.

Though it is not solely 'about' religion, *Narrow Road to the Deep North* does demonstrate through the interaction of its characters, how deeply-rooted religious belief can cause immense political and personal tragedy. Bond describes the play as a comedy, and it *is* very funny, but it is also shocking and surprising. The shock and the surprise are, however, filled with a clearly functioning intelligence, and the play asks for an understanding response from its audience. It is characteristic of all Bond's plays that humour and surprise establish a context in which the audience can use its head, with its feelings also engaged.

The play tells a story of epic proportions, lasting over thirty years and encompassing the rise and fall of a whole city state. Set in Japan, "about the seventeenth, eighteenth or nineteenth centuries", the play has a short introduction which is a fairly exact dramatisation of an incident in *The Records of a Weather-Exposed Skeleton*, by the 17th century Japanese poet, Matsuo Basho. He is a leading character in the play, and in the introduction he tells us who he is, what he has done ("I . . . brought the haiku verse form to perfection and gave it greater range and depth . . .") and what he's about to do (". . . I'm going on a journey along the narrow road to the deep north and when I reach there I shall become a hermit and get enlightenment.") The play goes on to outline Basho's involvement in a vast series of historical changes concerned with the rise and fall of the Emperor Shogo, tyrant ruler of a city state who rules with the ruthless cruelty of a Ghengis Khan. Basho is so outraged by Shogo's behaviour, but especially by his disrespect for religion, that he persuades a British Expeditionary Force to intervene and colonise the city. Shogo leads a counter-coup, but it is short-lived, and the city remains in western hands. It is a story which obviously reflects the forcible westernisation of Japan at the turn of the century, when the country became just another market for expanding imperial Europe and America, a process which had been going on ever since the Portuguese arrived there in the 16th century. This great weight of political history finds expression in the actions of the characters, and it is the various choices that they make or fail to make that move the narrative forward.

Religion lies at the heart of Bond's telling use of surprise in the three characters who constitute the play's three main centres of influence. They are Basho, the Buddhist poet, Shogo, who is a despairing non-believer, and Georgina, the Christian missionary/politician. All the other characters, peasants, priests and soldiers, fall under the influence of these three characters, and their peculiar delusions. Basho introduces the play, and within a page or so he is presented with a crucial moral choice. By the end of the play, we will know just how devastating are the consequences of this choice. By the end of this scene, though, we at least know Basho's reasons for choosing to do what he does. Meeting two starving peasants who are abandoning their baby on a river-bank because they don't have enough food to feed it, Basho notes the problem, but makes no effort to help. This is how he explains his inactivity: "It hasn't done anything to *earn* this suffering – it's caused by something greater and more massive: you could call it the irresistible will of heaven. So it must cry to heaven. And I must go to the north." (It was at this point in reading Basho's journal, that Bond was so affronted by the writer's moral stance that he felt unable to read on, and the play was conceived.) Basho, like all the believers in the plays, locates the centre of his being outside himself. By deciding that he must give priority to the religious virtues of ego-denial and desire-denial, Basho opts out of the material world and leaves a baby to die of exposure and starvation, whereas for Bond, the protection of life is an absolutely fundamental instinct rooted in human identity. To ignore that instinct, he shows, is tantamount to committing suicide, and in the play's final scene, a younger, more impressionable person does just that. Basho is a poet as well as a Buddhist, and the impulse which moves him to seek spiritual perfection also makes him yearn for artistic purity. That too is something which Bond resents, because artists have been the traditional developers and communicators of human-centred values (often, ironically, when making art about religious ideas). So, Basho goes to the deep north, spends twenty-nine and a half years staring at a wall and comes to the unsurprising conclusion that he'd already known everything before he went there. Now he is presented with another choice. A young man, Kiro, whom he meets at the same spot on the river where the baby was abandoned, wants to become a disciple, because the priest who brought him up told him to become the disciple of someone who had got enlightenment. Basho is contemptuous: "You're not ready to be a disciple, you don't know the first things!" He advises Kiro to join the local seminary. That action, or rather inaction, also contributes its small stream to a widening river of misery and disorder that flows from Basho's first refusal to engage with the world.

Basho's next major involvement in the story also concerns choices. It begins with a scene which modifies what has, so far, been the sombre tone of the play. Five priests, now including Kiro, come along a road carrying a religious relic, a pot in which an ancient Emperor once hid. Instead of being complacent and smug, like Basho, these religious men are like children, and like children their innocence has about it something vulnerable and fragile. Their hopscotch and leapfrog-playing, singing and dancing around the sacred pot, is both light-hearted and emotionally direct. Note the stage directions: "There is a subdued, relaxed, amused murmur . . . . Argi cries for a few seconds in annoyance. Then there is a contented, amused silence." Their simple joys are curtailed when Kiro sticks the pot on his head and can't get it off. Basho comes along, like an adult spoiling the children's game, but he can't think of a way to get the pot off, and neither can the other priests, whose innocent gaiety is seen after all to be a luxury – when it comes to solving problems like stuck pots. Imprisoned, as Kiro is physically, inside a religious relic, they become anxious and mystified, and impotently defer to

Basho. Later when Georgina 'converts' them to Christianity by issuing
regulation tambourines and clerical collars, they behave like spoilt children,
ingratiating themselves with the 'adult', one more sign that their innocence is,
of itself, fairly useless. "Can I bless people? . . . And tell them they're born
evil?" shouts Argi stupidly.

Basho is again forced to make a choice when he and the still-imprisoned
Kiro turn up at the Emperor Shogo's court, and once again religious belief
determines the movement of the scene. It is a scene of astonishing and
violent contrasts. The atmosphere of terror politics is established with the
sudden, staggering entrance of the Chief Police Inspector, a spear, intended
for Shogo, stuck through him. Shogo goes on to tell Basho he must care for a
baby, the son of the old deposed Emperor, giving him the easy choice of the
baby or being thrown in a sack into the river. Now, in one of those
characteristic Bond scenes where two strongly contrasted but linked incidents
take place on stage, Shogo smashes the holy relic to release Kiro, and shoves
a peasant into the drowning sack. Shogo's whole relationship with society, his
attitude to power and to religion, is brilliantly conveyed by Bond in this one
sure theatre image. Basho is so outraged by this sacrilege that he is forced,
out of Shogo's hearing, to articulate his own religious philosophy: "But how
can I hope if he destroys religion? He knew the pot was sacred. Of course,
that's only a symbol, but we need symbols to protect us from ourselves." It is
true that Shogo's city is hell, but Basho's analysis of the problem is based on
the premise that religious symbols are more important than human lives. His
next act is to organise the violent overthrow of the old regime by enlisting
British military intervention. Once the British enter the arena, Basho's role
becomes less significant. Although he is puzzled and somewhat contemptuous
of the Christians, they are at least religious, and anything is better than
Shogo's militant agnosticism. Equally important, perhaps, they *are* the new
ruling power, and the means for his advancement. He therefore becomes a
functionary of the occupying regime, ending finally as the state's poet laureate
and apologist. His first act in the play had been to leave a baby to die. His
last act is to participate in the public execution of Shogo, who almost certainly
was that baby, by delivering an oration in which he declares that he should
have killed the baby there and then. Now made Prime Minister, Basho
declares that with Shogo's death "The sin is broken!" The religious idiom is
clear proof that events in the play have reached the logical and terrible outcome of the mystic's pursuit of perfection outside himself. He has betrayed
his own ideals and his own identity.

Religious thinking is also crucial to Shogo's character, even though his only
god is Shogo. Through his relationship with Kiro, we begin to see that
what motivates Shogo is despair, and a human-centred despair at that (a
neat irony when we have been led to criticise Basho because his world is
God-centred). Shogo declares that he does not love God, and his reason for
ruling by atrocity is that "life makes people unhappy, not my city." Though
he sets no store by God, his actions show that he sets no store by humanity
either. His is the despair at the root of fascism. As the play progresses, it
becomes clear that he lives in a fantasy world that is as unreal as Basho's. "I
am the city because I made it, but I made it in the image of other men.

People wanted to follow me – so I had to lead them. I can't help shaping history – it's my gift, like your piety." Shogo is almost justified in making that comparison because both he and Kiro, the young man, have dedicated their lives to a dangerous ideal – Kiro, to God, and Shogo to a despairing idea of man. (It is quite within Shogo's expedient character, though, to dress as a priest to escape from the occupying powers, and con his way out of trouble by uttering obscurantist religious waffle at them.)

Exiled to the deep north, Shogo and Kiro continue to talk about themselves, and the more that Shogo reveals about himself, the more contemptuous he is of Kiro's belief: "You don't live, you sit and play with yourself and think of God!" Shogo opts in to life, where Basho opts out. He may not know what human beings need for their happiness, but he does engage with them, and with human society. By the next scene, he has organised a counter-coup, properly-armed this time with western munitions, and is now determined to kill the baby Emperor who has been the Christians' legitimation for ruling. Try as he might, he cannot make Georgina surrender the baby, and to be certain, he has all her infants slaughtered. What is remarkable about Shogo throughout the play is that he creates his own morality out of the chaos and despair of his own experience. We know from the play that he still misses his dead parents, that he knows that he was an abandoned child, denied love when he most needed it, and that he suffers from some unnamed and terrible guilt. It it any wonder then, that his morality is twisted and distorted? Nevertheless, it has about it traces of a human dignity, and in his desperate attempt to avoid slaughtering all of the innocents in Georgina's care, he achieves a kind of crippled humanity that is found by no other character in the play. His execution by the British is almost a parody of Crucifixion: "Shogo's naked body is nailed to the placard. It has been hacked to pieces and loosely assembled upside down." Like Christ, he is a sacrificed human being, but Bond surrounds the execution with the bleats of justice and religious fervour: "The head of the city has paid for his sin. The city is purged. Feed your eyes and rejoice!" He thereby places the execution in an overwhelmingly human context. There is no heaven for Shogo, and his death is the more terrible for it.

If the discovery of a warped dignity and a thwarted compassion in Shogo is one of Bond's most original paradoxes, the portrayal of the Christians is certainly one of his funniest. But whatever makes for humour in Georgina also presages madness for her, as her interwoven political and religious ideas combine to crush her. In this sharp-edged satirical portrayal Bond sums up the whole colonial and imperialist experience of Britain. History shows us that in Victorian Britain politics and religion became horribly mingled and were raised to a bizarre level of national fantasy (a fantasy to which Bond gives his own characteristic expression in *Early Morning*). Behind the extraordinary rhetoric typified by Lord Rosebery's exclamation during his Rectorial address at Glasgow University in 1910: "Do we not hail in this less the energy and fortune of a race than the supreme direction of the Almighty?", the Imperial Adventure was in reality the political/economic consequence of British industrial expansion. Once on that treadmill, the growing economy sought new markets, and given that the

Kiro imprisoned inside a religious relic. *Narrow Road to the Deep North* at the Northcott Theatre, Exeter, 1971.
(Photo: Nicholas Toyne)

The South African Prime Minister takes communion while his policemen murder black men. *Black Mass* at the Almost Free Theatre, London 1979.
(Photo: Bob Chase)

prevailing ideology was Christian, it was inevitable that a new fusion should come about, combining a renewed religious energy which fuelled the national will and a racist ethic which subdued any opposing political or religious structures. In a deft and caring characterisation, Bond embodies in Georgina both the brittle strengths and the tragic self-ignorance of British Imperialism.

One of Georgina's most telling characteristics is her lack of ordinary guile at least when she feels she is in the company of equals. She is quite articulate about her strategies, and is straightforwardly honest even when planning to deceive. Her eventual mental collapse comes about because her sort of aristocratic certainty can comprehend no possibility of failure or disaster, and it is her religious belief that fuels her faith in herself. Underlying her religious optimism however there is a very real threat of good, old-fashioned violence, so her response to Basho's request for help is:

> We will give you soldiers and guns to kill your enemies – and in return you must love Jesus, give up bad language, foreswear cards, refuse spicey foods, abandon women, foresake drink – and *stop* singing on Sundays . . . except hymns and the authorized responses.

These speeches are funny now because of the arbitrary triviality of Georgina's canons, but they are very untrivial in that they are about power and authority. Georgina's genteel lust for power leads her to appropriate for herself the area of activity where power can be most irresponsibly wielded with society's full blessing – the education of children: "In this suburb of hell they are all orphans of Jesus, and I claim them on his behalf. Hallelujah!" Her real delight is to replicate her own vision of the England she has left behind, a nation based on the ideology of religious morality. In one of the play's key speeches, she outlines to Basho the careful inter-relation she has developed between her desire for political power and her religious belief. In her mind, the two have become so richly confused that she sees no shame or contradiction in explaining herself to Basho in explicit detail: "So instead of atrocity, I use morality. I persuade people – in their hearts – that they are sin, and that they have evil thoughts . . . If sin didn't exist it would be necessary to invent it." There is obviously something nagging in Basho's mind about such explicit confidence. As if prophesying the disaster to come, he tells Georgina a Japanese proverb which she doesn't understand: ". . . people who raise ghosts become haunted."

Just as we are adjusting to the idea that Georgina is little different in practice from Shogo, the counter-coup arrives and she is stripped of all power. Thus exposed, she shows real human feelings. She hurries on with her five children and is confronted by Shogo, searching for the young Emperor. Her sanity has always relied on a fusion of religious faith and actual power, and now that power has been torn away, she clings to faith. Even as Shogo interrogates the children to discover who might be the child he must murder, she insists on the ritual proprieties and when the soldiers take the children out to murder them, she starts to sing a hymn. It is her last hope, and it fails her. The children's corpses are brought back and her sanity gives way. Like King Lear clutching Cordelia's corpse, her mind wanders around the ruins of her own destroyed certainty. Despite her prayers to God, the unspeakable has happened. Weaving in and out of the rambling pretence that the five little corpses are once more alive, there comes, like a taunting echo, the children's hymn:

> Naughty boys . . . Dirty hands . . . Nasty hands . . . Keep your hands still!
> Tight together! . . . Stop playing with your sins! . . . What comes to
> naughty boys? . . . (*She dances, plays the tambourine and sings.*) He gave
> them snow in winter . . . and lips that we might tell . . . all things bright
> and . . . dead . . . (*She plays and dances a few steps.*) . . . All dead.

It is the moment Georgina ceases to be a centre of influence in the play. Like
Shogo shortly after, she reaped the whirlwind of her dangerous fantasies.
Only Basho remains alive and well, of the three, and it was he who set the
events in motion by allowing a child to grow up without love.

The other characters in *Narrow Road to the Deep North* are mostly the
passive recipients of the political and social holocausts unleashed by Basho,
Shogo and Georgina. Bond creates, with remarkable economy, a line-
drawing of the class structures of both Japanese and British societies, from
the gullible Japanese monks to the cynical British soldiery hedging their
theological bets:

> . . . they could be on their way, in a manner of speakin', an' mention me
> in their prayers, which would be very 'andy – like if the unlikely ever
> 'appens an' I was t' go t' 'eaven and the Almighty turns out t' be a
> Buddhist an' not a Wesleyan after all.

It is Kiro, of all these more passive characters who is almost the most
important character in the play, because he is the one who is willing and
eager to learn and to change. Like Shogo, he lost his parents through
starvation and was brought up by a priest. He too is cut adrift from the
normal human expectations of love and protection. Kiro, though, has none of
the self-assertive need to act, to establish his identity by affecting the world,
of Shogo. He is gentle, contemplative, and prepared to learn from the
experience of others. When Basho refuses to be his teacher, he goes to a
seminary, but that doesn't satisfy him. His encounter with Shogo, who
smashes the holy pot from his head, is something radically different. The
tyrant and the monk strike up a relationship which develops into a brief,
mutually supportive friendship. Kiro becomes, in effect, Shogo's alter ego.
He hates the tyrant: "He should be beaten! He's a tyrant and god will
destroy him!" But he loves the man, and as the invading army comes nearer,
he tries to persuade Shogo to escape. In the deep north, Kiro is inactive and
contemplative to the point where he irritates Shogo, and when Shogo
organises his army to recapture the city, Kiro won't fight with him. The next
time they meet, Shogo is in chains after the failure of his counter-coup. Kiro,
who learnt little from his religious training, placed his faith in a man of
action, and now has to witness his death. As the execution ceremony
proceeds, he reads some of Basho's scattered poems. Like Georgina, he has
placed the centre of his being outside himself, and, like Georgina, he now
sees the object of his faith destroyed. The final scene brings together, in one
richly resonant piece of theatre, the four characters who have played major
parts in the play. Basho the poet, lately Prime Minister, reads the execution
oration. Shogo is publicly dismembered and Georgina, her mind now an
insane tangle of religious and sexual guilt, imagines that she is about to be
raped, as the gentle Kiro disembowels himself because he has no inner

resources with which to combat his despair. It is a telling irony. Kiro, superficially the most attractive character, opts out of the world by committing suicide. The play's final image stands as a massive question mark over that act: as Kiro carefully cuts himself open, a man clambers up out of the river that has featured in the lives of all the characters. "Didn't you hear me shout?" he says to the dying Kiro, "I shouted help. You must have heard and you didn't come . . . I could have drowned."

By creating actions which give breath and flesh to moral problems faced by people everyday, Bond not only asks questions but creates the artistic material from which each member of the audience might be able to start forging answers. Human beings are forced to respond to whatever their society presents them with, and it is these moments of choice, to accept the status quo or not, that are symbolised by Basho's actions. Whatever Bond's intellectual doubts about religion it is the weakening of the natural human tendency to engage with, and create anew, human society, that *Narrow Road to the Deep North* confronts. In one interview, Bond says: "In an ideal society, he [Basho] would have picked that baby up gone off the stage, and there would have been no necessity for a play."[7] For Bond, religion is a long-established mechanism by which human beings may evade responsibility for their own, and other people's, lives.


Bond's argument with religion, carried on consistently throughout *Narrow Road to the Deep North*, emerges in some form in every one of his plays to date. In the quasi-naturalistic plays, *Saved* and *The Pope's Wedding*, Church institutions are just the decayed outbuildings of modern bourgeois society, now only conceivable as the object of dirty jokes. Both plays envision worlds where a lifeless religious morality is violated by the true nature of the society it seeks to protect. As if wishing to home in on the history that has caused that morality to come into being, Bond next embarks on *Narrow Road to the Deep North* and *Early Morning*.

*Black Mass* and *Passion*, Bond's first two short plays written for specific political movements, proclaim their religious preoccupation in their titles, Both, indeed, feature Jesus Christ as a main character. *Black Mass* takes place in a church. The Prime Minister of South Africa takes communion while outside, his soldiers and policemen massacre demonstrators. When he and the priest leave the church to fraternise with the victorious troops, in a stunningly deadpan *coup de theatre* Christ nips off the cross and poisons the communion wine. Instead of guying or parodying Christ, in both this play and in *Passion* Bond responds fully to the human figure on the Cross, while Christ as a spiritual figure is shown as a character to be pitied, his holiness as a retarding affliction. The communion-wine poisoner is detected by an alert police inspector who wants to arrest the offender, but the priest, mindful of scandal, decides to ask Christ to leave. He pours forth a stinging lecture on responsibility: "It's not fair on others to allow someone like you to continue to be in a respectable institution like this. Go, and I hope you find somewhere you can fit in. Have I made myself clear?" Christ, who says nothing throughout the play might, at this stage, seem like the quasi-revolutionary Jesus of some Latin American church. On the other hand, there's a playful truculence discernible in the stage directions which suggests someone rather more wayward: "Christ leans against the cross in boredom ... . Christ hangs one arm over the horizontal bar of the cross." These movements, taken with the character's silence, and the readiness with which he leaves the church, undermine the heroic possibilities.

Christ in *Passion* is a more serious-minded gentleman. He arrives in a post-holocaust wilderness, with Buddha as a faithful sidekick, to find various English ruling-class characters chatting about how to build a facsimile of the society which has just destroyed itself. While these are delightful caricatures of very dangerous people, Bond again searches out the human, fallible and therefore dignified dimension of Christ. In steady, resigned prose, he talks of coming crucifixion: "I must die soon so that the world may be healed." This is the conventional Christ, dying for men's sins, but when they arrive at the Cross, there is already a victim nailed there. It is a pig, a despised domestic animal, yet it expresses both the grotesque cruelty of the punishment and an earthbound, physical image of suffering. (This image probably owes something to the painting 'A Slaughtered Ox' by Rembrandt, an artist for whom Bond has enormous admiration.) Christ's reaction to the pig is to despair. Surrounded by insane rulers and their suffering subjects, he concludes that all humanity must be mad, certainly beyond his help: "I can't be crucified for men because they've already crucified themselves . . . How can one innocent die for the guilty when so many innocents are corrupted and killed?" Christ and Buddha, gentle people both, and agonised guardians of Good, are well-meaning incompetents, quite unable to cope with the material problems of humanity.

Having so thoroughly anatomised religious belief in *Narrow Road to the Deep North*, *Black Mass* and *Passion*, in the plays that follow Bond allows priests and religion to take their place in a wider social pattern as one of several elements in authoritarian societies. Bond's criticism of religion is thorough and yet curiously yielding. His achievement has been to create theatre which is Marxist in that his characters are the products of social processes, whose motivations and actions find their energy in social relationships. This doesn't imply a simplistic or determinist idea of human nature. On the contrary, Bond is a playwright who reconstitutes the idea of Free Will for human beings, and his fundamental objection to religious belief is that it takes responsibility away from human beings. It is, in its way, an ecstatic conviction. Bond is so impressed by the unrealised potential in human nature that idea-systems like religion which devalue Man before God, serve only to smother alarming and beautiful energies. The Parson in *The Fool* turns his thoughts to death when events round on him, but Bond's plays urge us to resist despair, to take responsibility for our own lives, and to create the societies that will make that possible.

# 3:THE WORLD

If, in Bond's human-centred vision, religion is a fantasy or an evasion or a tool of power politics, then the world into which we are born must be above all a material one. People's lives are not, in Bond's work, divorced from their natural environments, like actors in the Georgian theatre walking about in front of painted trees and avenues. Much of the suffering and misery that his characters undergo occurs precisely because their social lives have somehow lost contact with their existence as elements of the natural world. "We evolved in a biosphere," writes Bond, in the *Lear* preface, "but we live in what is more and more becoming a techno-sphere." In this chapter, I want to look at the way the world of nature – the landscape, animals and the biological instincts of man – is used to sharpen our awareness of the structures that limit human freedom.

Few modern dramatists create landscape quite as vividly as Edward Bond. Most dramatists who criticise and analyse society usually prefer to concentrate on a world dominated by technology and man-made objects. Pinter or Wesker, for example, will lavish great care on interiors, detailing props, costume and furniture, but Bond, who *can* do these things, will more often be creating precise outdoor settings. He is, perhaps more than any of his contemporaries, an outdoor playwright, making of the English landscape, even in cities, something individual and powerful, possessed of its own life. Nature is important not as decoration for the action but because Bond sees there the objective evidence for his own moral sense.

Apart from *Saved*, most of his plays take place in the country, or in small towns, and they concern themselves with the class politics of country communities. *Saved*, though certainly one of the classic plays of city life, is a play in which nature is conspicuous by its absence, or by the feeble imitations of nature invented by people. Some of its most important scenes happen in a park, a bureaucratically-ordinated imitation of the country for the town poor. In the park there is a pond, an imitation river or lake, for people to fish in. It's hardly surprising that this literally un-natural setting should become a place of menace and threat, where the un-natural boredom and frustration of the young men in the play finds its outcome in child-murder. (It was perhaps no accident that, following *Saved*, Bond was hired to script Antonioni's *Blow-up*, a film which powerfully conveys the strangely menacing quality of English urban parks.) Bond himself has spoken of the world of *Saved* as "the brick desert, and the feeling of being in a desert of bricks seemed to be absolutely right for the play".[10]

Natural things in the plays are more than simply metaphors for something else. Images like a desert or a sea or a ditch do suggest other levels of experience, but they usually have an immediate physical reality too. When characters use these kind of metaphors in speech, they are reacting to an environment that is sharply real for them.

Country life seems to occur so frequently in Bond's work because of his family's history of farm-labouring, and also because of those periods of wartime evacuation which so sharpened his responses to the country. Since 1966, Bond has lived in a village near Cambridge, and his work now draws on that environment, just as *Saved* drew on his experience of the city: "I didn't choose to write *Saved* about a particular place or in a particular dialect. That was the way I talked, and the kind of setting I was familiar with. I now talk rather differently and live somewhere differently . . . so it would be artificial for me to write another play like *Saved* now."

I have claimed that few modern dramatists evoke landscape as well as Bond. *Lear* shows just how vividly he can draw a landscape without burdening the scene with a specific geography. Thirteen of the eighteen scenes take place out of doors. In the open air, outside man-made buildings, man and nature become part of the same system. Even in cities, it's difficult to avoid wind, rain or sun, and the less well off you are, the more you will feel the wet and cold, and be grateful for the sun. Bond does not set up a man-against-nature conflict, but man as part of nature against man as the slave of abstract social devices, such as money.

The landscapes of *Lear* are drawn with remarkable economy. The opening scene – *Near the wall* – swiftly sketches in the physical setting.

COUNCILLOR. Isn't it a swamp on this map?

FONTANELLE. My feet are wet . . .

LEAR. Who left that wood in the mud? . . . It's been rotting there for weeks . . . They treat their men like cattle. When they finish work they must be kept in dry huts. All these huts are wet.

After Lear's fall, the stage directions shift from the muddy squalor of a building site to the woods, and the house of the Gravedigger's Boy: "*Wooden house upstage . . . A well.*" Later scenes show "*Prison convoy on a country road*", "*Near the wall. Open fields*", "*The wall. Steep earth bank.*" In other scenes, the landscape detail is still further refined. Both the rebel army led by Cordelia, and the Royalists under Bodice and Fontanelle wander round the countryside, each as lost as the other: "We never come straight an' the maps is US", says one soldier. "I was born in the city. These fields are China t' me."

In a handful of stage directions and lines of dialogue, Bond creates in *Lear* a flat, open landscape, but one capable of sustaining life. It is, in fact, very similar to that East Anglian countryside in which he spent important parts of his childhood and in which he now lives. Indeed, the wall in *Lear* was suggested by the massive earthworks near his home called Fleam Dyke and Devil's Dyke, thrown up by the East Anglians after the departure of the Romans to protect themselves from marauders. Stretched between forests to the east and fens to the west, these huge walls are still visible for miles around, although they are cut through now by roads. The dykes have a hard grandeur, running for miles across flat, wet, rich-soiled farmland cross-hatched by drainage ditches. Such a landscape, through which flow gentle rivers, is prone to flooding and one of its most common man-made structures is the bridge.

Both bridges and floods recur frequently in Bond's writing. Bridges carry people safely over danger, but they are structures vulnerable to attack both from nature and from Man. They are therefore symbols both of safety and threat. Bond's characters often use a bridge to define some meeting-point between safety and danger. In *Early Morning*, Arthur's mental landscape, for instance, is fear-ridden: "I don't go near rivers when the bridges are burned. They look like the bones of charred hippopotamuses." For Albert, they confirm his own despairing ideas of human nature: "Every time you open a bridge you know people will throw themselves off it." For Lear, they confirm his experience of the treachery of life: "I once knew a man who drowned on a bridge in a flood." For the Old Woman in *Bingo*, a bridge is a way of mocking Shakespeare's evasive complacency: "Start buildin' bridges when your feet get wet." When Shakespeare is forced to decide about the enclosure issue, he thinks of the decision as a river. But the crafty Combe defuses the danger involved in river-crossing: "We needn't build a bridge if there's a ford downstream." A ford is a bridge for cheats, and Combe knows that moral cheating is what Shakespeare wants to hear.

Flooding, too, carries a similar ambiguous charge. Rivers swelling beyond their banks, transforming the landscape into inland seas and temporary lakes, are both threatening and beautiful. The myth of the Flood in Genesis gives to the natural event something of the historical force that popular thinking now sees in the idea of Revolution, a time of vast change, of revaluation, and sometimes of widespread death. The Old Woman, for instance, thinks of the seven good years she had with her husband as "Time 'fore the flood." In *The Sea*, where huge elemental forces threaten to overwhelm a small, inward-looking community, Evens warns Willy that the body of drowned Colin might not be washed up again by the fickle tides: "Don't count on it. There might be a flood. Then everything goes by the board . . ." He goes on to tell a haunting little parable about a man drowned at sea and washed inland by a flood which left him hanging in an apple-tree in his own garden, watched by his stranded family. Floods invade the cosy familiarity of things, levelling everything to a sea. But seas were once the source of all life. *The Sea* opens with a huge storm which is as fruitfully violent as a difficult birth. The opening stage directions indicate: "Masses of water swell up, rattle and churn, and crash back into the sea. Gravel and sand grind slowly. The earth trembles." At the play's end, Evens refers back to this tremendous natural event: "I believe in sand and stone and water because the wind stirs them into a dirty sea, and it gives birth to living things."

If seas of water are the breeding-ground of life, then that life is often sustained by rivers of water. Rivers occur in Bond's plays as mute witnesses to all that human life undergoes. In *Narrow Road to the Deep North*, a river is the place where Basho ignores an abandoned baby, where, thirty years on, he makes his home, and the place where Shogo drowns innocent peasants. Beside another river in the deep north, Kiro and Shogo talk, and beside the river in the south, Basho regrets not drowning the baby while the adult Shogo is publicly dismembered. Finally, a new man, wet as from birth, stumbles half-drowned out of the river to chide Kiro's corpse for not helping him. A river is, as might be expected, a dominant image in the opera libretto *We Come to the River*. It is a place where children and old people are murdered by soldiers, an imagined place of refuge for the inmates of an asylum, and finally, the symbolic barrier to freedom that the oppressed victims have to cross: "We stand by the river/If there is a bridge we will walk over/If there is no bridge we will wade/If the water is deep we will swim/If it is too fast we will build boats/We will stand on the other side/We have learnt to march so well that we cannot drown." But this affirmation of human possibility is not allowed to stand naively unqualified. As the dead victims sing of their power, the living victims, mad men and women, cavort in white sheets, imagining that they have found rest and peace in a river: "O the water is clean and cold and pure! How beautiful I am! Beautiful! Beautiful! Beautiful!"

The river that has flooded and threatens to drown the peasants in *The Bundle* is seen to have a political meaning in that the landlord uses its natural power as a threat which he can appear to counter with paternalistic care. Only when the peasants take his power from him and control and direct the river's power are they safe.

A river is central to *The Fool*, but here it has a very precise economic reality, and therefore plays an important political role in the action. Bond weds two pieces of history – the life and madness of the Northamptonshire poet John Clare, and the nineteenth-century food riots in Cambridgeshire – in order to seek out some origins of our own culture and society. Linking these two histories is the idea of culture, meaning both the creative work produced by a society and the organising principles of that society. In *The Fool*, both sorts of culture are rooted firmly in the land, and the play shows the destruction of both. The old relationship of man to the land decays not merely because a new technology makes possible enclosure, drainage and factories, but because industrialisation brings with it a new intensification of class relationships. For men and women living in the Fens of East Anglia, life before drainage was undoubtedly hard, but it was feasible. The Fens provided food for all in the form of wildfowl and fish, and drier land was owned by no-one, so cattle could be grazed more or less anywhere. When the common land was fenced in by the new landlords, and the Fens drained to create more fields, landowners became possessed of a rich source of income. The poor were simply dispossessed. The justification for all this legalised robbery was Efficiency; and if yield per acre of crops is the only criterion, then enclosure and drainage probably were efficient. In practice, of course, the real results of the changes were that the poor became totally dependent on the land-owners who paid wages. They became, in effect, slaves. The Parson, in his Christmas address to the Mummers, offers a landowners' policy statement in the opening scene:

. . . But we are entering a new age. An iron age. New engines, new factories, cities, ways, laws. The old ways must go. The noble horse and the plough are so slow. Our land must be better used. Forest cut down. Open spaces put to the plough.

The Parson, who in effect hi-jacks the cultural celebration of the land-workers, expresses the optimistic, progressive, nineteenth-century excuse for change, whereas Lord Milton's hard economic analysis shows another side of the coin: "Wages follow prices or civil institutions break down. Civilisation costs money like everything else. Put too much in your own pockets and what's left to pay for our State institutions?" In this opening scene, Bond digs straight down to the political roots of a society on the point of change. Again, the river crystallises the interaction of man and nature because the river and the fields which it periodically floods, are what keeps most of the population from starvation. So when Milton begins to drain the Fen (in Darkie's pungent phrase, "to turn off the river"), he threatens their lives or at least their lives as something other than slaves. He also plans to cut down forests to sow corn – not so that the community might profit, but in Darkie's words "to sell t'the old factory boys. They on't grow corn." (The idea of enclosure as a pattern for the robbery of a people's energy and resources haunts several of Bond's plays. It is the issue in *Bingo* on which Shakespeare is to be judged. It is the mainspring of *The Fool*, and there is almost a pre-echo of enclosure in *Lear* where peasants dig up the wall which squats infertile on their land. In a sense too, *The Pope's Wedding*, which is permeated with the facts of poverty in the rural working-class, is about the persistence of that same exploiting system of land-work that we see begun in *The Fool*.) Lord Milton's plan heralds a new age where nature and natural relationships are reduced to abstracts. Patty puts it in her own terse poetry: "They saw chaps gooin' round the fields this mornin' with chains an' writing books. Thass how it all come out. Wrote the river down in the books." Darkie half understands the changes that are about to overwhelm them, but in doing so, he plays into the hands of the landowners: "They take all the land, they'll hev t'pay us proper wages." Clare understands the full implications but he has no idea how to cope with them: "We'll lose our fishin' – our wood – cows on the fen common. How'll we live? Not on the few bob they pay us for workin' their land. We need us own bit a land."

In *The Fool*, the picture of a drastically-changing rural culture grows increasingly varied and subtle. Having shown how important the land is economically, Bond goes on to develop a marvellous series of self-deluding characters, each of whom claims to understand the land. The Parson, stripped and humiliated by rioting peasants, is shaken into sombre reflection which a certain limited truth, but is in fact only self-deception: "How small and impotent we are. We clear a few fields, build a few houses, twist a few rods of iron, and think our lives are everlasting . . ." On the other hand, we have the absurd idealising of Mrs Emmerson, walking Clare in Hyde Park (a place of violence like the park in *Saved*): "See, Mr Clare, we have grass and trees in this park. Do they not inspire you? O, to be touched by the wings!" Even when she gets out to Clare's village, she fantasises: "It's as I imagined. Full of peace and stillness . . . Surely he can find peace in this garden?" Lord Radstock burbles on about Clare's "fine love of English landscape" but ticks him off for radicalism. It is typical of Bond to create ruling-class characters who fool themselves, their lives soured because their money isolates them from reality. Both Mrs Emmerson and Lord Milton descend into a bitter and regretful old age. Milton, visiting the insane Clare, talks about his son, whom he has grown to hate: "A vicious bastard . . . Don't see much of him except his back. Busy. In love with his factories. It's changed." Milton can't see that

The peasants, trapped by floods, bargain for places in the landowner's boat. *The Bundle,*
R.S.C. at the Warehouse, 1978

'Where is the beast? The blood is as still as a lake.' Lear looks for sin in his daughter's
entrails. *Lear,* Last Knockings Theatre, Company, Leeds 1972.
(Photo: Tony Coult)

his son's behaviour is the result of his own creation of a new industrial age in which the twin imperatives of production and money corrode personal relationships. Only the victims of these new conditions begin to understand what is going on, and of them, only Patty survives the play. Darkie is hanged for fighting the new order, and his mates deported in prison ships. Clare, who has written about the misery and contradictions of the new order, goes mad. Even the Irish navvy, who realises "If they bring any more machines on the land, they won't need us", has moved on. Patty alone has the extraordinary strength to survive, but it is the calloused toughness of someone who has suffered much. Bond's poem about Patty concludes: "If asked she would say/ I make do with what I have and go without what I haven't/And no man can snap her." She is the only character apart from Milton able to react to the startling changes that transform Britain in her lifetime, but it is a passive and impotent reaction. "Come by train" she says to the living corpse of her mad husband. "There! You on't bin on a train with all your gaddin' about. Line goo by the village. Goo out Sunday evenin's an see the trains. The sparks doo goo. There!"

Weather, too, is a function of the natural world, and sometimes plays a significant role in Bond's plays. In *The Woman*, for instance, one of nature's most destructive acts, a waterspout, shipwrecks the Greeks with their cargo including Hecuba, Ismene, and the statue over which the terrible war had been fought. The whirlwind of water represents a material force with its own logic and sense which contrasts with the religious belief in the statue held by Heros and generally with the slave-culture of Greece.

Weather, and its effect on the landscape, becomes a touchstone by which it is possible to judge human actions. As much as Heros is trapped by his religious fatalism, so is Nestor trapped by his divorce from the rationality of nature: "Waiting on the wind and sea – that's not the soldiering I understand".

When the winter storms hit the island, they are the natural equivalent of the man-made storms that smash societies of men and women. Hecuba, however, tells the Man not to be afraid of their violence, the same paradox that occurs in the poem *Seasons*:

"How gentle, the terrible seasons come and go . . ."

The far more destructive storm raised by Heros in his absurd pursuit of the Trojans, and of the statue, results in his own death at the hands of the miner. Hecuba's death at the hands of the storm, on the other hand, comes after a temporary resolution of the crisis in the play, and after she has played her part in creating that resolution. The storm does not complete the sequence of actions, however. It will return again, and there will be more storms, season by season. In the same way, Hero's death is not an end. It is a beginning, for the miner, for the islanders, and ultimately, for the audience.


Bond writes about the past in order to discover the causes of present problems, so many of his characters live in societies where nature and the animal world are far more prominent in people's lives than they are now. Animals in technological societies tend to be simply pets, or factory products, and increasing numbers of us have no sense of animals as a normal part of the environment. One possible result of that loss is that we have a diminishing sense of ourselves as animals, and we are thus led into distorted views of what our real needs and pleasures are. While recognising the danger of blandly applying data about animal behaviour to human beings, Bond insists that animal and human needs are closely related. So, in his Preface to *Lear*, he writes: "Our human emotions and intellect are not things that stand apart from the long development of evolution; it is as animals we make our highest demands, and in responding to them as men we create our deepest human experience."

Violence, as anyone who has followed Bond's career will know, is what Edward Bond tends to be known for. Some critics still pretend that Bond loves the violence he presents on stage, and the only possible explanation for such an aesthetic misreading can be that those critics are reading in something of their own neuroses. As if to counter that kind of error, Bond wrote in the *Lear* preface a clear statement of his reasons for writing about violence: "Violence shapes and obsesses our society, and if we do not stop being violent, we have no future. People who do not want writers to write about violence want to stop them writing about us and our time. It would be immoral not to write about violence." Bond's thinking about violence owes a great deal to the work of those anthropologists he has read, particularly on the nature of aggression in man and animals. This reading has provided him with the theoretical confirmation of his own feelings on the subject. If in fact Bond is mistaken when he says that "There is no evidence of an aggressive *need*, as there is of sexual and feeding needs", then his plays really are only entertaining nonsense. If human beings do have an innate aggressive instinct, then it follows that human nature is flawed, or sinful, as the religious mind would have it. If Bond is wrong, then we must accept the need for tougher punishments, greater discipline and control, all imposed from above by people who are our 'betters'. Such is the consistency of Bond's playwriting, and the importance of the things he writes about, that if he is wrong on this basic point of human nature, his plays really do fall apart. The ideas that he attacks all share a deep despair about human nature, which is often labelled 'animal nature' as if that were some kind of denigration. In *Bingo*, the Son spits out his disgust at his father's fucking with the Young Woman in the orchard: "Hev yo' no shame? God an' man see you in the daylight. Yo 'm drag creation down t' the beast. Animal. They ugly ol' legs. Runnin' loike a thief. Ugly." If, on the other hand, human beings are not aggressive, as Bond would say the evidence shows, except "when we are constantly deprived of our physical and emotional needs, or when we are threatened with this", then we are led to question what it is that deprives and threatens us. The answers will be social and cultural, and the problems will be solved only by political action. So Bond digs right back to the basic motives that drive all human activity. Acknowledging no gods, he looks to nature and the material world as our only source of self-knowledge.

Bond's plays are full of the imagery of animal life, particularly, and not surprisingly in view of its Shakespearean source, *Lear*. Animal imagery charts both the mental landscape of the King, and the changing society in which he operates. For the first production at the Royal Court in 1971, the poster and programme graphics showed a caged monkey, back turned defensively to the observer, and that represents something of Lear's position as a prisoner both of his own illusions and of the revolutionaries who take power. Scene One shows a confident national leader inspecting the wall, dealing with order and discipline. He complains that his men are treated "like cattle", not because they have no freedom, but because the huts they are kept in are damp. "You waste men," he tells the Foreman. His daughters' suitors, dukes from other kingdoms, are threats: "They'll be like wolves in the fold", and his people are "my sheep, and if one of them is lost I'd take fire to hell to bring him out". It is the imagery of a rural culture, and it is the language of a King who sees his subjects as less than human, an image of them which is deeply patronising because Lear imagines he loves his people.

When his daughters throw him out of office, a great change starts to take place in Lear. Plunged into an agony of self-appraisal, he begins to see himself as an animal, but his self-images are self-pitying, as they must be for this man who has always fooled himself: "I am a famished dog that sits on the earth and howls", and "My daughters turned a dog out of its kennel because it got fond of its sack". In his attempt to understand what has happened to himself, Lear uses desperate little parables in which animals appear as victims in landscapes of fear, or as creatures in some Grimms' Fairy Tale: "The mouse comes out of his hole and stares. The giant wants to eat the dragon, but the dragon has grabbed the carving knife." Lear's consciousness in these passages is at its most self-dramatising and melodramatic, and the imagery matches this with visions of terror, death and emptiness: "The wolf crawls away in terror and hides with the rats" . . . "I slept in the morning because all the birds were dead." Then as Lear begins his slow climb back to sanity, his vision begins subtly to change. In the trial scene, Bodice gives her father a mirror to pitch him still further into madness, and although he sees his own reflection, he characterises it as "a little cage of bars with an animal in it. (*Peers closer.*) No, no, that's not the King!" The agonised outpouring that follows shows him, in the cauldron of new perceptions, shifting the focus of his pity from himself to an image which mingles himself with some undefined tormented animal: "There's a poor animal with blood on its head and tears running down its face . . . Is it a bird or a horse? . . . Who broke its wings? Who cut off its hands so that it can't shake the bars? It's pressing its snout on the glass." In the next scene, Lear's mind has conjured up the Ghost of the Gravedigger's Boy. Lear has gone 'mad', but he can now hold the animal-image at a distance so that it begins to control the horror of his new experience: "There's an animal in a cage. I must let it out or it will be destroyed." In the moment of relative calm brought on by the fantasy entrance of Bodice and Fontanelle as children, Lear returns to a time when he might have changed the course of history, or, at least, of his own history. The moment of stillness prompts from him an idealistic vision of peace, in which the animal/Lear finds hope: "The animal will slip out of its cage, and lie in the fields, and run by the river, and groom itself in the sun, and sleep in its hole from night to morning." But the vision is Utopian, and when the unreal daughters leave the stage, the dreadful present bursts frenzied back into his imagination. He thinks he hears an animal scratching:

"There's blood in its mouth. The muzzle's bleeding. It's trying to dig. It's found someone", and he collapses unconscious.

From now on, Lear begins to feel and understand the sufferings of other people. In the profoundly affecting autopsy scene, Lear has to watch the prison doctor "making a few incisions to satisfy the authorities" in the dead body of his daughter, Fontanelle. As he sees her guts, he is overwhelmed by their natural order and beauty. It is, of course, a terrible, almost ludicrous admiration because only a hugely-violated body can be seen in that state, and only a mind in some bizarre extremity could find beauty in such a sight. Yet Lear does, and finding no "beast" to blame amongst the "bits and pieces packed in with all that care", he is able to understand his own responsibility for his daughter's death. His animal images are now quite objective, and the animals themselves have changed: "She sleeps inside like a lion and a lamb and a child." After the final horror of blinding, Lear is again plunged into the search for meaning, and begins now to use nature as a yardstick against which to test his own experience: "All life seeks its safety. A wolf, a fox, a horse – they'd run away, they're sane." He has now begun to come to terms with the experience of suffering inside his own mind, because he knows what suffering is, and how much he has caused, and so he uses a parable about a bird to teach others what he has learned. The story tells of a bird trapped in a cage and later crippled by having its wings broken, thanks to human vanity and cruelty. In the penultimate scene, Lear answers "Yes" to the Ghost's question: "Can you hear an owl on the hill?" but "No" to "But not the fox?". The owl is a conventional symbol of death, so although Lear's final wish is "to live till I'm much older and become as cunning as the fox", the imagery anticipates events rather than his wishes. As the scene ends, the Ghost, companion and tempter, enters, gored to a second death by the pigs he kept while alive. Finally free of the dangerous compromising of the Ghost, Lear's last reflective statement offers us a new image of himself as a thing of nature. This time he sees his whole life, not as an animal, but as a tree: "I see my life, a black tree by a pool. The branches are covered with tears. The tears are shining with light. The wind blows the tears in the sky. And my tears fall down on me." This new perception, in which Lear sees his life as something deathly, sad and yet now curiously serene, illustrates the distance he has travelled in the play. The circularity of the image – tears blown into the air and falling back on himself – precedes a final breaking-out of the self-destructive circles in which his life has always moved.

I have tried to show some of the ways in which Edward Bond uses facets of nature to illuminate the experience of being human. However, there is no 'back-to-nature' naiveté in this, and the Ghost shows how dangerous are those escapist fantasies of rural life which threaten to cut Lear off from the pains and sorrows of wider society. Scopey tries to do this; and it is one of Mrs Emmerson's middle-class fantasies. One of Bond's best poems, *Seasons*, which appeared in the programme of the first Royal Court production of *The Sea*, contrasts the natural violence of wind and weather with some of the work of human hands. On the one hand: "The iron vice of anger/That holds its threat for generations/The frown that becomes its own repose . . ." and on the other: "The black storm/Ice shattering its skull at night/Flood carrying tree roots at its head –/These are the mild seasons". Another poem insists that even in the magnificence of the natural world, we have still to be actively human in it. The poem ends: "All the oceans cannot contain one tear/All space cannot silence a laugh/All the conjuror's spells cannot create what is normal." The barriers that prevent an actively human life in an organic world have to be removed. For Bond, those barriers will always be political.

# 4:SOCIETY

> I do think freedom is philosophically and actually possible. And my own
> judgement is that free societies will actually be created. I don't think
> people will be satisfied with anything else.
>
> Letter from Edward Bond to the author, 24 March 1975

Edward Bond has written much – whether as introductions to the plays,
programme notes, or other articles and journalism – which sets out a 'deep
structure' of ideas informing his theatre, and while his plays inevitably begin
from an imaginative seed, an image or a cluster of words, there is nevertheless a consistent view of society and its discontents embodied in the plays,
one that is best summed up in Bond's own phrase: "rational theatre". There
are few more severe critics than Bond of the uses of modern science, but his
idea of rationality is basically a commitment to scientific method. Bond
presupposes, like a doctor examining a patient, that what happens in societies
has identifiable causes, and that things can be done to effect change when
that seems necessary. "The future *is* choosable, and it's malleable, we *can*
form it, we *can* have what we want", he said in one interview.[14]

In the struggle to find a way of living that accepts "the need to love,
create, protect and enjoy", many of Bond's characters find themselves in
more or less bitter conflict with a society based on classes. Class oppression is
a fact of life, even, it must be said, in the affluent liberal democracies of the
West, where the mythology is that class conflict can be muted by reform to a
point where it is nothing more than spice to the spirit of healthy competition.
The reality of the myth is shown in a play like *The Pope's Wedding*. Bond has
explained that he saw the shape of a cycle of plays which was to end in *The
Sea*, even before he began *The Pope's Wedding*: "I would begin with a
tragedy in which the old man would not talk. This boy called Scopey keeps
saying, 'Why do this?' And the old man can never say anything. He just
drools. Scopey never gets an answer from him. I wanted to end the series of
plays with two people sitting on a beach after the storm has died down,
talking to an old man. They try to come to terms with the problems that they
have to face."[17]

*The Pope's Wedding* is set in Essex, the nearest area to London that Bond
could reach to research, and it seems to gain much of its conviction from his
own experiences of the rural working class. From the outset, the play shows a
world dominated by money. The characters are all young working-class
people for whom the absence of money is one of the determining facts of
life. The first scene takes place on Thursday, the day before pay-day, the low
point of the week. There are few ways of escape from the situation, so Byo's
reaction to the suggestion that Bill has been at it with the boss's wife is "Yoo

stan' a doo yoorself a bit a good". Bill's jokey and frustrated "Let's goo an' burn a yank" fills in the canvas by establishing the atmosphere of rural superstition and isolation (which, in the past, would have led to witch-burning), as well as opening up the possibility of Alen's persecution. It is also a reminder that East Anglia has seen, from the Second World War on, a mushrooming of US Air Force bases. The presence of all that thundering, destructive technology amongst closed and isolated communities must have been perceived locally almost as a kind of black art, practised by affluent aliens, who were, in effect, twentieth-century sorcerers.

These lads still have connections with the fruitful traditions and habits of the past. Ron's "I oiled that owd Ferguson this mornin'. Yoo should a seen 'er. My life!" might be about a tractor, but it also says that craft pride still exists, even semi-magical practices like Lorry's hanging his scythe in an apple tree "t' take the rust out on 'er". Nevertheless, running like a thread through all their talk is money. Bill would sell his sister for a fag, and Byo keeps business-like account of those he's lent to Ron. The first thing anyone says to Pat and June when they enter is "Lend us five bob". After the tug-of-war in which her handbag is broken, Pat is hurt by the attack on her privacy and dignity, but the subsequent row is conducted in cash terms:

PAT. Now yoo buy a new one.

SCOPEY. I ent buyin' nothin'.

PAT. Yoo pay up or I come round yoor 'ouse . . .

JUNE. Yoo won't think that's cheap when you see the bill.

Pat's parting shot is "You'll pay, don't worry", and Byo's reply to Bill's "I ont gooin a get no loan off 'er tonight" turns the metaphor sexual: "See what yoo *can* get." Money, though, has to be worked for, and the scene ends with the fact of labour: "Up in seven hours", says Ron. It's closing time, so that means getting up at something like 6 a.m.

Scene One shows us the texture of living. Scene Two begins to fill in the agencies that impose that texture, and one of these is the man who employs the farm workers, Mr Bullright. He doesn't appear, but exerts a powerful influence on the early part of the action. A local cricket derby is to take place, one team made up of the farm workers, the other including Bullright. Although Ron talks about cricket as "strength and skill and guts", there are more devious things going on, because Bullright intends to stop Bill from playing by keeping him on the farm to tend a sick animal. Ron guesses that it's just a tactic to ensure that Bullright retires from the captaincy victorious, but Bill knows he can't refuse to work: "There's plenty waitin' for my job, boy." On the other hand, he doesn't accept it lightly: "(*Twists his scythe.*) I'd like t' 'ave 'is owd 'ead stuck on this." That verbal violence is transposed into a sexual key: "I'll bloody well lay 'is missis for a start. I'll grind 'er, for one." Mrs Bullright is Mr Bullright's property, and Bill's laying her in revenge is like smashing his windows, or setting light to his hay-ricks.

In these two opening scenes, Bond describes in precise social detail a community from which meaning has to be snatched where it may from the bleak possibilities offered to its members. Bullright holds almost feudal authority as the local employer. His workers, on the other hand, are restless and energetic, but unclear how to use their energy, and so they wrestle with each other, bickering about money and beer. By Scene Two, they can look forward to a class confrontation, but it is symbolic rather than real. Scopey is the only person to profit from it. So far, he's just been someone else in the group, but Bullright's perfidy offers him, quite by chance, an escape route. He just scrapes into the team to replace Bill, but on the day, he plays a blinder, winning the match for the workers. He also wins Bill's fiancée. After the match, while a victory party goes on in the pub, Scopey and Pat make love outside. "Yoo look beautiful all in white", she tells him afterwards. It has been an amazing day for Scopey. Suddenly everything seems to go right. His tragedy, though, is that he doesn't have the resources to make that happiness last. Life has shown him possibilities, but even before his day of triumph is over, the social limitations begin moving in to crush him. As the scene ends, the other lads, having 'defeated' Bullright, want to get Alen, the old hermit whom Pat looks after. They have tasted the energy of rebellion, but they don't discriminate, and going for the helpless is at least one way to feel that they have some effect on the world.

From now on, the action begins to impinge more and more upon Alen, and he upon Scopey. Alen is a man who has become a scapegoat, which is why he, in turn, has gypsies for his own scapegoat: "Dirty owd diddies scratchin' be me door". Despite a hint of an affair between Pat's mother and himself, he has always been outside society, rootless: "My mum an' dad moved all over. We always stopped just outside places. We were the last 'ouse in the village . . . I never stopped gooin' after people. They stopped gooin' after me." Meanwhile, Scopey begins to criticise things around him, as if searching for some way to re-experience his day of happiness. When Pat and June look at a postcard from a friend in America, now married to a US Serviceman, Scopey criticises its unreal colour: "Yoo need more than that. Yoo'd 'ave t'see more . . . Where yoo seen streets like that? Nothin's like that. No more yoo ent seen sky like that . . . Where's the people an' the corners?" But Scopey's search for some kind of meaning gets side-tracked. The girls cope with a life they don't see as particularly changeable with a tough, witty fatalism: "If it 'ent corns it's piles", says Pat. Scopey, however, looks for his salvation in Alen who offers him a challenge, an object to patronise and exert power over, but also a symbol of a kind of romantic freedom – alone, unattached, self-governing. But it is a deceptive freedom, not least because Alen relies totally on other people to bring him food, fuel and domestic comforts.

The tied cottage that Scopey and Pat move into is almost as run-down as Alen's, another indication of their economic deprivation. The only hope of escape is to move to " that new estate be Dunmow", but there is no money for a deposit, so Dunmow is as impossible a dream as the city on Betty Legs' postcard. Scopey's distraction from a bleak home life is to substitute himself for Pat in caring for Alen. At first, he treats Alen rather as a nursemaid would treat an awkward child. Deprived of any other means of asserting his identity, Scopey patronises Alen by cooking for and feeding him. He oscillates between threats – "Yoo want me t' fetch the police? They'll put yoo in the institution right away" – and a rough, adequate caring – "If that tastes as good as it smells, yoo'll be all right". He begins to articulate for himself what attracts him to Alen: "No worry. No one t' nag. My wife'll be wonderin' what I been up to. Yoo ent ever married, 'ave yoo." Slowly Scopey becomes trapped between a fantasy life, which he identifies with Alen's social isolation, and his own home life, which is for both partners just another kind of isolation. At home, everything is predicated on scarcity, and on very private property. Scopey hoards his overtime, there's no milk or cocoa when it's wanted, they argue about who has smoked whose fags and, finally, about who owns the water for a cup of tea. They both use property to establish some kind of desperate identity. Having no future, Scopey uses Alen to look for a life in the past. Everything about the old man speaks of the passing of time – the flyblown photographs from an old scrap-shop in Dunmow, the old army greatcoat, the rumours that, in the war, he was "flashin' secrets 'a the Jerries with a Woolworth's torch". But it is all a false solution to Scopey's problems, and he begins to suspect as much when he realises that Alen uses the mysterious pile of newspapers, not for "his work", but just to stand on to look out of a spy-hole in the wall. Alen, like the pockets of the greatcoat, is empty for Scopey. Disappointed, yet still mystified by his fantasy of the tramp outside society, he kills the old man and attempts to take on his personality by wearing his coat and living in his hut. Meanwhile, in the outside world, things have returned to 'normal'. Bill bids to win back Pat, and one of his attractions is that he's now got cash enough to put down a deposit on a car. The workers lose the annual cricket match. Scopey's flight from the pressure of being poor in an affluent society (he is a "nomad wandering around inside an oasis", as Bond describes the Irishmen in *The Fool*) is a flight out of reality, something not to be believed, as much a fantasy as a pope getting married.

In both *The Pope's Wedding* and *The Sea*, a character finds his life thwarted by a rigid class structure, and in both plays, he attempts to find some way out by going to an old man in the community, an outsider, a tramp. (The odd spelling of Alen and Evens might even be taken as evidence of their link.) In *The Sea*, Bond's portrayal of a class society is wider in scope. Where the landowner in the earlier play is only referred to, here there is a clear, threefold class structure, similar to that in *The Cherry Orchard*. Mrs. Rafi is the traditional centre of power in the town, the lady to whom money means little because she has always had it. Hatch, however, the aspiring bourgeois struggling to set up his own business, is desperate to the point of madness about money, while men like Hollarcut have no independence at all, and are treated like disobedient children. In *The Pope's Wedding* the emblems of a pseudo-democratic capitalist state are things that are cheap and shoddy, things like Pat's handbag which Scopey complains "won't stand up t' proper 'andlin'", Lorry's broken TV set, the wiring in Scopey's place which is "US" (possibly both unserviceable and American?), or the junk in Alen's hut. Compared to these, the props in *The Sea* are very much up-market. If the stuff in the earlier play comes from junk shops and Woolworth's, the merchandise in Hatch's shop is the very finest that he can obtain from the wholesalers in Birmingham – velvet curtains, Nottingham lace, Giupure

D'Art, Turkish carpets, Japanese nainsooks. Scene Two resounds with these exotic labels, building up an oppressive sense of stuffy 'quality', while all the time reminding us where wealth actually comes from. Mrs. Rafi, determined at all costs to keep Hatch under her thumb, complains "I'm not interested in this new-fangled craze to support the trading efforts of the Empire by getting the east coast into native dress", and the reiteration of *Indian* dhurries, *Turkish* carpets, *Japanese* nainsooks, further defines the tight relationship between commerce and the Empire.

The main class conflict in *The Sea* is between Mrs. Rafi and Hatch, and what brings it to a head is the corrosive influence of commerce on human relations. Hatch is already plagued by paranoid visions of men from outer space coming to invade the earth, but the continuing servility of his business relationship with Mrs. Rafi eventually drives him very much more mad. Her refusal to accept the velvet curtains she had ordered triggers the collapse of his sanity, but not before he has attempted to communicate to her the psychologically precarious position of the small businessman:

> I'm in a *small* way of business Mrs. Rafi. I'm on the black list. I had to pay for all this before they sent it. And I made such a fuss about delivery. All my capital has gone into it . . . I couldn't set up in the larger towns. No capital.

He belongs to that class which has often been the first to support populist right-wing politics, and Bond's writing analyses why.

The conflict between Hatch and Mrs. Rafi is won by neither. Hatch goes off his head, trapped by the contradictions of his professional life, and Mrs. Rafi comes to realise that it won't be long before she will be senile and hated, and therefore treated as if she were mad. Indeed, the only people who can escape madness are the two survivors of the storm that killed Colin. His friend Willy and his lover Rose are both open to change, and to learning. It is to Evens, the man outside society, that Willy turns for help, but the decision does not turn to tragedy as it did for Scopey. One reason for this is that both Willy and Evens are conscious of their own confusions and problems. Evens warns Willy: "Don't trust the wise fool too much. What he knows matters and you die without it. But he never knows enough." If Alen was a total dead-end for Scopey, Evens perhaps has something to offer Willy. Bond describes the ending as "a celebration of articulacy". It shows Evens, the self-conscious, dying outcast helping the unformed younger people to cope with a world in which he has failed. Some critics complain of Bond's naiveté in the speeches about the rat-catcher, but these speeches can never ring wholly true because Evens' life is, in its way, shallow and self-regarding. It is of the utmost importance to Willy that he admits as much: "I'm a wreck rotting on the beach. Past help. That's why I live here out of people's way. It wouldn't help *them* if they lived here. We all have to end differently." Bond does, however, admit some degree of naiveté in trying to make the play end differently for each member of the audience by finishing it in mid-sentence. In this sense, it is, formally, Bond's first participatory play!

What we have seen so far are some of the ways in which Bond shows the destructive effect on people's happiness of a capitalism whose deepest values are non-human and whose methods of working are therefore unjust. However, both *Narrow Road to the Deep North* and *Lear* warn that pre-capitalist and post-revolutionary societies can destroy happiness just as effectively if they do not break fully with the inhuman values of the past. Bond's plays are about change, and how the need for change is to be recognised. Evens' last words in *The Sea* – "Remember, I've told you these things so you won't despair. But you must still change the world" – paraphrase these of the Chorus in Brecht's *The Measures Taken*: "Sink into the mire/embrace the butcher/but change the world." Changing the world at the speed and in the direction that Bond would want is a process of socialist revolution.

Talk of revolution in Britain these days invites paranoia or ridicule. There are many reasons why this should be, not last the vested interest of all the comfortable members of society (and the comfortable nations) in keeping things as they are, even at the expense of discomforting other people (or other nations). In view of the relative failure of countries like Russia to effect a socialist revolution, why should Bond still urge revolution of some kind in the affluent liberal democracies of the West? The Cambridge critic Raymond Williams in his book *Modern Tragedy* offers this forceful statement of the necessity for revolutionary change, and of its essential humanity:

> A society in which revolution is necessary is a society in which the incorporation of all its people, *as whole human beings*, is in practice impossible without a change in its fundamental form of relationships. The many kinds of partial 'incorporation' – as voters, as employees, or as persons entitled to education, legal protection, social services, and so on – are real human gains but do not in themselves amount to that full membership of society which is the end of all classes . . . Revolution remains necessary in these circumstances, not only because some men desire it, but because there can be no acceptable human order while the full humanity of any class of men is, in practice, denied.

That statement expresses the spirit of Bond's desire for change. He might want to add that it isn't only principles or desire that demand revolution. It is the threat of total human extinction posed by advanced weapons technology that makes the problem so urgent. In a newspaper interview, he said: "The problems facing modern man have become simplified and austere. They amount to the question: Can the human species survive?" [8]

Bond is not a playwright of political tactics. A writer such as Trevor Griffiths by dramatising the clash of different progressive ideals addresses himself more to the particular problems of how *precisely* to make a revolution. *The Comedians*, for instance, in the scenes between Waters and Price, is a debate about two kinds of left-wing thought in the language of a debate about comedy. Griffiths says: 'My plays are never about the battle between capitalism and socialism. I take that as being won by socialism.' Bond's political debate, however, starts one step further back. His plays tend to be set at moments in their characters' lives which ask the questions 'How do we *decide* that change is necessary? How do we even become *aware* of what is going wrong?' They are concerned with how the conditions – personal and social – for change are arrived at, and therefore all deal in some way with the politics of learning and education, for it is here that we are encouraged or discouraged to use reason to analyse the world, and imagination to change it. If, as children or adults, we learn badly, social change might stagnate or go into reverse. If we learn well, social change has a fighting chance of being both radical and humane.

Bond's own experience of the education system was, to say the least, uninspiring. Considered too stupid even to be entered for School Certificate at his secondary mod. in Crouch End, he left school at 15. "That was the making of me, of course", he writes. "You see, after that, nobody takes you seriously. The conditioning process stops. Once you let them send you to grammar school and university, you're ruined."[4] He once rather flamboyantly declared: "I think that universal education is one of the worst disasters that has hit Western society since the Black Death . . .", which he went on to justify: "I'm not against knowledge, I'm against training, against indoctrination, against regimentation. Our schools are like prisons. There's really no difference between our state prisons and our state schools."[8] Bond mistrusts formal education because it is authoritarian – *We* educate *you* – and sets it apart from the active process of learning – We learn *from* you, or *about* these things. As well as the implied criticism of our educational institutions to be found in *Saved* or *The Pope's Wedding*, many of the plays use the process of learning as a structural principle. 'Education', writes the critic William Walsh, 'begins with the particular, goes on to theory in the widest sense, namely the study of structure and organisation, and concludes again in a heightened sense of the particular.' That three-part structure occurs again in Bond's own description of *Lear*: "Act One shows a world dominated by myth. Act Two shows the clash between myth and reality, between superstitious men and the autonomous world. Act Three shows a resolution of this, in the world we prove real by dying in it." *Lear* is, then, a play about political education. It is in the gradual realisation that his actions have consequences for him, as well as for his victims, that Lear's learning takes place. To use Walsh's description, his life while he is King, is governed by a very limited idea of the particular, then the sufferings of deposition and betrayal compel him to the study of the structure and organisation of political power. Finally, his new perceptions give him a heightened sense of the particular with which he can finally take action to put things right. His tragedy is that it is then too late for him to do anything but teach a handful of younger people, and then face inevitable death.

One of the most contentious issues in revolutionary argument must be the use of force first to make revolution and then to sustain it. This issue is tackled by Bond in *Lear*. The play is about the tragic nature of history, particularly revolutionary history, and it is tragic because, as Brecht said, 'The sufferings of this man appal me because they are unnecessary'. Those who oppose change, even for the noblest reasons, usually see the tragedy and the suffering only in the *act* of revolution. However, as Raymond Williams again points out, 'The violence and disorder are in the whole action, of which what we commonly call revolution is the crisis'. In other words, violence is woven firmly into the fabric of society long before revolution comes along to tear it apart. The peace enjoyed by Shakespeare in *Bingo* is full of violence because it cannot be separated from the violent society outside his walled garden. This whole action is seen at work in *Lear*. The King shares responsibility not just for the political situations which he sets up, but also for the actions of his daughters, who rebel against him, and for the revolutionary Cordelia, who rebels againts all three. This structure of cause-and-effect operates throughout the play. The soldiers and labourers in the first scene are part of a machine created by Lear to protect his kingdom from attack. In so doing, he creates slaves by forcing men from their homes, families and livelihoods to build the Wall. The wall that defends society becomes a prison wall that confines it, and this structure of oppression reaches back into history: 'I killed the fathers', says Lear 'therefore the sons must hate me. And when I killed the fathers I stood on the field among our dead and swore to kill the sons.' Lear doesn't understand that using terror to protect 'his' people from foreign injustice and aggression simply ensures that it thrives at home. His passion for isolation is born of a fatal, sentimental misunderstanding of his own power which he passes on like some hereditary disease to his daughters. Even before Lear asks himself the question "Where does their vileness come from?", Fontanelle has already suggested the answer. As she and her sister are left alone, their plans for the overthrow of their father's regime hardening, she says: "Happiness at last! I was always terrified of him."

The idea of actions being determined by their social and personal context is continued in the character of Cordelia. Faced with the violent disintegration of the old regimes of Lear and his daughters, she has to fight a guerilla war in order to seize power. During the fighting, she orders the execution of a captured soldier while one of her own guerillas lies dying from a stomach wound, declaring: "When we have power, these things won't be necessary." When she does have power, she uses terror to silence her enemies Bodice and Fontanelle, and she restarts work on building the Wall. Herself a brutalised victim, she sets out the guidelines which allow the carpenter to have Lear blinded. This dreadful measure is supposed to make Lear politically impotent. Its actual effect is to give him further insight into the political process: he becomes a nuisance to the new regime, a dissident who has to be stopped from talking to people. Cordelia tries to stop him involving himself in public affairs, and finally confronts him to ask him to back down. It is a very telling scene, with Cordelia, who watched the soldiers kill her husband and then rape her and who saw her child miscarry, defending the rebuilding of the Wall in order to create a just and free society: "I said we won't be at the mercy of brutes any more, we'll live a new life and help one another." Lear is a threat to her vision of a just world, but he will not be silenced, and he pleads with her to restore humanity to the revolution: "You have two enemies, lies *and* truth. You sacrifice truth to destroy lies, and you sacrifice life to destroy death. It isn't sane . . . Our lives are awkward and fragile and we have only one thing to keep us sane: pity, and the man without pity is mad." But Cordelia, whose own sufferings, heaven knows, give her the right at least to argue, sees in this only self-pity (as do some left-wing critics of Bond's position generally). There are things Lear doesn't know about, and there is, after all, something rather comfortable about criticising

Class society: young farm-labourers the day before pay-day. *The Pope's Wedding*, Northcott Theatre, Exeter 1973.
(Photo Nicholas Toyne)

Class society: the town gathers for a funeral organised by Mrs Rafi. *The Sea,* Royal Court Theatre, 1973.
(Photo: John Haynes)

from the sidelines while others do the work. Nevertheless Lear, too, has suffered, and in the end, he does what he can, knowing that Cordelia will have him disposed of, by digging up the Wall with a spade, in a symbolic gesture which may just act as an example to the younger people who have listened to him. Cordelia's boast, "We'll make the society you only dream of", is determined, courageous and principled in its way, but she will never make a revolution that will, in Lear's words, at least reform.

Cordelia is, it must be remembered, the daughter of a priest, and she has always been defensive and unhappy when her own security has been threatened, so that she wants Lear turned away when he first takes refuge in the house. Bond shows us the social roots of the unhappiness in Cordelia so that we can begin to understand her decision to allow a limited terror. In his Preface to *Lear*, he cautions against the political activist's tendency to vanguardism: "If your plan of the future is too rigid you start to coerce people to fit into it. We do not need a plan of the future, we need a *method* of change."

The problems of revolutionary violence suggest another reason for the importance of education to Bond and his characters. This is the possibility that education affords to establish the widest possible consensus that things are not right and need changing, and that only humane socialism has any hope of doing so. The more people that see the necessity for change, and demand it, the less opposition there will be, and therefore the less chance that change will be violent. In the end, though, Bond does not take up a simple pacifist position. A new Preface to *Saved*, written for Volume One of the collected edition of his plays, emphasises and summarises three major points about violence and society: 1) There is no evidence of a human *need* for violence, and the idea that there is is a myth perpetuated because it makes political control more easy; 2) Human nature is determined mainly by interactions between the individual and society. It is not innately 'good' or 'bad' but is a product of the culture that people live in; 3) There is violence in most so-called stable societies, as much as in unstable ones. (This is the principle behind that evocative invitation to a Sunday Times interviewer: "Walk out with me in the open air, and I'll show you something unforgiveable.." [4] ) Audiences who see the plays have, like Willy and Rose in *The Sea*, or Susan, Thomas and John in *Lear*, to confront the unforgiveable things in society before deciding what to do, and the action they take may yet, tragically, have to be violent as long as there continues to exist a violence that is socially acceptable: violence of class, of authoritarian teaching and of the deprivation of human rights: "Reason is not yet always effective, and we are still at a stage when to create a rational society we may sometimes have to use irrational means. Right-wing political violence cannot be justified because it always serves irrationality; but left-wing political violence is justified when it helps to create a more rational society, and when that help cannot be given in a more pacific form." This action has to be the result both of necessity and of calculation. Wang has to bite his lip till blood flows to prevent himself crying out ineffectually against injustice. He calculates here that action would be ineffective. When Hecuba in *The Woman* hands the Dark Man a sword, on the other hand, the time is ripe. The demands of the man's experience are united with the woman's understanding of political structure and design. "This is your only chance" she says, judging the moment but impotent to act because of her blindness. "I only need this" says the man taking the sword from Hecuba and acting on her judgement, under the protection of her tactics, to kill Heros.

In *The Bundle,* Bond sets out to deal with some of the problems of revolutionary activity. "There *is* a true morality," he says in an interview, "but in a class society like ours, that's not the one that becomes part of the law. One of the things I've tried to do in *The Bundle* is to demystify the use of moral argument so that we can't be morally blackmailed any more." The story of *The Bundle* springs from the same incident in one of Matsuo Basho's travel books that prompted Bond to write *Narrow Road to the Deep North.* In *The Bundle,* the baby left to its fate at the river's edge is rescued by a ferryman, who cannot afford yet another mouth to feed, yet takes pity on the helpless child. The child grows up to be Wang, whose life is moulded by his experience of injustice. When the river floods and traps his parents and neighbours on the high ground of the local graveyard, he is forced to sell himself into the landowner's service to buy himself and his parents a place in the rescue boat. When his enforced apprenticeship is over, he leaves the security of the court, meets up with a gang of bandits and begins to teach them about the politics of the situation in order to mould them into a guerilla army. Eventually, the overthrow of the Landowner's power is accomplished, and his natural ally in terror, the swelling river, is contained and controlled by cut-off channels and earth banks.

The play's moral pivot is the extraordinary scene in which Wang, now a young adult, finds another baby bundle by the river. He has to choose to leave it there, as Basho abandoned him, or to rescue the child as he himself had been saved by the ferryman years before. To rescue the child would mean that all his energies would be expended feeding the two of them. To abandon it, in effect, to kill it, would allow him to work to change the society that condones the murder of children by neglect. "Is this all?" asks Wang, "one little gush of sweetness and I pick up a child? Who picks up the rest? How can I hold my arms wide enough to hold them all? Feed them? Care for them? All of them? Must the whole world lie by this river like a corpse?" He calls the child a "little killer" which threatens to neuter him politically, and thus to condemn hundreds more babies to death. Shaking with the injustice of this awesome and apparently insoluble contradiction, Wang holds the baby in the air, and in a denial of one of his deepest instincts, hurls it into the river.

Wang's action is not offered to us for our moral appraisal. It is, rather, a theatre image which illustrates with a terrible clarity the moral contradiction forced upon him, and on the play's audiences, by unjust social systems. The babies rich Western society chooses to ignore strew the world, and Bond, through Wang, demonstrates the absurdity and danger of charity as a response to mass starvation.

"You have to change society structurally", says Bond, "and in order to do that, you may find yourself involved in doing what is "wrong". This idea is embodied in *The Bundle* and contrasts with Cordelia's actions in *Lear.* As a guerilla soldier lies dying, she says, "When we have power, these things won't be necessary," but when power is in her hands, her regime is repressive and cruel. This is not a pessimistic theatre statement, however, simply a cautionary one. The contradictions that face Wang and Cordelia can only be resolved by the exercise of critical judgement and analysis. "You can't lay down absolutes," says Bond, "and say 'Be guided by this.' It's also not a question of understanding what the end is, so that the end justifies the means. We have to understand that we are people in a process and we have to understand where we are in that process now in order to understand where we arrived from. If you understand the situation, then instead of saying "We want happiness and peace", you understand the realities of these things, you work for those objectives. It's not a Utopian vision. It comes from understanding where you've been and what your situation is now. That's why history plays have been very important to me."

While every Bond play is in some sense political, all of the short plays and the opera libretto have been *overtly* so. The first fruit of his collaboration with the composer Hans-Werner Henze, the opera libretto *We Come to the River*, is a reworking of some of the themes of responsibility and political power of *Lear*. Bond chose to use material with which he was familiar to leave himself free to concentrate on technical problems like the three-part staging. The script which the composer received is a remarkably condensed piece, set in "Europe; nineteenth century or later". It tells the story of a victorious general who is told by his doctor that he will go blind. The news makes him consider the suffering he has caused, and so he begins to subvert the ruling order. The governor of the province has him put in an insane asylum, where he is approached by both the governor and a dissident soldier to act as figurehead for the respective movements. When the soldier assassinates the governor, the general is implicated and the emperor arranges for him to be blinded. The play ends with all the dead victims of state terror returning solemnly to the stage while the inmates of the asylum smother the general who, though blind, **threatens** their spurious peace. While the Mad People play in a fantasy world, **the** resurrected dead make their own claim for eventual victory through the strength and determination of all oppressed people. The sense of hope, achieved despite terrible suffering, in this final anthem, must answer those who query Bond's faith in the possibility of a successful revolution, or in the possibility of any human progress at all.

To date Bond has written five short plays on commission from various political and Alternative Theatre groups: *Black Mass, Passion, Stone, Grandma Faust* and *The Swing*. Their range of subjects has not been so unusual for a left-wing writer – racism, nuclear weapons, homosexual liberation, law and order – but the range of styles and approaches *is* remarkable, as is the way that these specific issues are related to the wider political context. Indeed *Stone*, which Bond wrote for a company which expressly uses theatre as a weapon in the struggle for homosexual liberation, makes no specific reference to homosexuality at all. In the programme note to the play, Bond emphasises the indivisibility of all politics:

I believe it was Einstein who said a society's level of civilisation could be judged by its attitude to anti-semitism. Later this was said about capital punishment. We could now say it about homosexuality – except that there are so many things it could also be said about.

A stone is given by a Mason in a business suit to an "eager and relaxed" young Man. The Man has to deliver the stone to the Mason's house, when he will be paid. The journey on which the young man embarks provides him with several strange encounters. Bunyanesque characters try to trick him out of the seven talents – Prudence, Soberness, Courage, Justice, Honesty, Love and Hope – given to him by his parents, or to corrupt them into seven deadly sins. Once the commitment to the Mason has been entered into (and the Mason has a gun to consolidate the agreement), the Man's journey becomes, literally, more and more burdensome, because the stone grows and grows until it is a huge rock chained to his back: "I cry at the stupidity of my life. Wasted on dragging a stone to somewhere I don't know for a reason I can't understand." Having at last fulfilled the terms of his contract by dragging the rock to the Mason's house, he is finally allowed to meet his employer, who answers his questions "Why did the stone grow? . . . Why did the coins change?" with evasions and the charge that he is a trouble-maker. The Man then kills the Mason, who in the best capitalist tradition has attempted to buy off the Man's militancy: "– the enterprise needs new management. You're our sort. (*Wheedling*.) I applaud all this. Initiative. It's time for a change. The new men are – (*The Man kills the Mason*.)." The stone symbolises all the burdens, of which homosexual oppression is but one, that are the product of the master-slave (latterly employer-employee) relationship. Talents are corrupted and life made miserable for the Man until he takes steps (and in this play, note, violent ones) to rid himself of the exploiter.

*Grandma Faust*, the first of the two short plays in *A-A-America!*, adopts a similar stylistic approach to deal with the subject of racism. The play is set in an unnamed southern state of America, and the literary model is more Brer Rabbit than Bunyan. Bond sets the racism of the American deep south within the framework of a cheerful folk-tale that makes daring use of racial stereotypes, black and white. Paul, the black man, is a simple fellow, with reasonable needs: "I'm hungry, suh. That's how I know I'm alive. Day I stop feelin hungry I know I'm dead." Gran ("A cross between Whistler's Mother and Grandma Moses") in her wheel-chair is, in fact, the Devil, and wants the black man's soul. She sets Uncle Sam up to do the catching, but there's a problem. Paul is *too* simple, that is, he is generous, a little gullible and certainly at a great social disadvantage. As Gran says: "He take such pity on me – bein old in a wheel-chair an puttin on I'm hungry – I keep gettin these terrible terrible waves of lovin kindness well over me." Paul is starving, and Sam's celebration of the loaf he uses as bait is mouth-watering:

Nigger, you're saliverin so bad my loaf is startin t'blush. That's a white loaf, boy, with feelings . . . She's succulent. Like bread ought t'be. Sweet an wholesome as mother made it . . . You don't use t'touch no white hand, you ain never gonna touch no white woman – but you can *swaller* my white loaf.

The play's action now develops into a struggle between the native wit of the black man, whose simplicity is now seen to be full of intelligence, and the devious manoeuvrings of Gran and Sam. Each time the bad guys seem to have the soul, the good guy slips out of their grasp. Finally, Paul and Sam fight a soul-fighting match in a cage. They use Paul's soul, represented by a doll, to hit each other with. Sam fortifies it with a lead truncheon supplied by Gran. Paul is nearly battered down, but at the last minute he hurls the soul out of the cage, and Sam won't chase it: "You know I ain never been out of the cage my whole life! Git wind an everythin' else out there." Gran wheels herself out in a frenzy of disappointment, and Paul is left standing fishing in the river where we first met Uncle Sam. He sings about his new freedom:

Little silver fish for my soul an me
Dancin together in the bright blue sea
A golden apple bouncin on the tree
Pick it an eat it an' you will be free.

*Grandma Faust* is, in the best sense, an entertainment, a clever and witty fable which joyfully satirises white American philistinism and self-regard and the crude racism which they foster. It makes an effective, and rather necessary curtain-raiser to its companion piece, *The Swing*, one of the most appalling of Bond's plays, and one of his very best. It is appalling because it is written around a historical incident (the very word seems indecently feeble) described in the prologue by another Paul, who although not exactly the same character as that in *Grandma Faust*, is also the only black in a white world:

In the fall of nineteen eleven in Livermore Kentucky a black man was charged with murder. He was taken to the local theatre and tied to a stake on stage. The box office sold tickets accordin to the usual custom: the more you paid the better you sat. The performance was this: people in the pricey seats got to empty their revolvers into the man. People in the gallery got one shot. An pro rata in between. Course he died very easy compared t' the style of some lynchin's.

Bond uses this incident to analyse the political roots of America (*The Swing* is subtitled "A documentary"). The inspired central image is the theatre building itself. An old vaudeville entertainer, Mrs. Kroll, has sold her theatre, a stop on the now defunct vaudeville circuit, to an energetic local merchant, Mr. Skinner. He intends to turn it into a store to catch the mining boom that is about to transform both the town, and everything else in the Wild West. Society is at a historical crossroads, moving from the old desperate individualism of the Frontier, into a new, expansionist stage of capitalism. The only future for culture and education here is a shotgun wedding to commerce, so Mr. Skinner persuades Mrs. Kroll's daughter Greta to take his son Ralph in hand: "I'd like him taught so's he can carry on like you did jist now – bout civilization an so on. If he came out with that he could sell a real classy line of goods." Greta, full of academic high culture, uses her learning as a buffer between herself and the world outside (she is perhaps what Mrs. Rafi is later to become): "We live on the border between civilization and barbarism. Which way shall we go? Do we know the answer? . . . Here in this quiet town, hidden behind the counter of a general provisions merchant, is a young soul yearning to be touched, opened, freed." There is a truth in this, but it is not the one that Greta imagines. Ralph is not the dying Keats figure with the sensitive face that she sentimentalises, but

Skinner's son, and therefore a personality wrecked by his father's over-bearing, philistine personality. Greta introduces him to Virgil, despite Skinner's insistence that he only needs fancy English to sell goods. But what flows between them as they sit around the parlour oil-lamp is not the wisdom of the ancients, but a vibrant current of sexual tension. In the frigid moral climate of small-town life, the spirits of the two young people are crushed by neurosis. In a scene alive with a suppressed and guilt-ridden tenderness, Greta's reading of Virgil to Ralph stumbles into agonised silence as she takes her breast out of her dress for Ralph to see, but not to touch. Ralph is terrified, and fascinated, but the moment of fondness dies because there is no letter of the social code by which they live that will allow them to touch each other, physically or emotionally. Shortly afterwards, Paul comes in with a lamp, and his presence reinforces their guilt. Shortly after that, there is an explosion of activity. Skinner's shop is attacked, he is wounded in the arm, and in the general confusion someone, or so she claims, touches Greta on the breast in the dark backyard.

Earlier, a young white man, Fred, who has been introduced to the new technology of electricity by Paul, celebrates his new diploma. He plans to open up an electrical repair shop, and even, despite Paul's rueful cynicism, to take his black friend on as a repair-man. Because of the words of the prologue, and because Paul is the only black in the play, it seems certain that when Skinner, his brusque humour now soured into righteous savagery, hunts for the culprit who broke into his store and attacked his daughter, Paul will be made the scapegoat. In the event, he seems to accuse both Paul and Fred of what has, in the sexually volatile moral climate, escalated into a brutal rape. The hysteria and moral fantasising mount, and they lead, inexorably, into the acting out of the events described in Paul's prologue. With the actual audience as unwilling substitutes for the historical spectators Mrs. Kroll once again steps out on to the stage of her old theatre, temporarily restored to its former glory, to warm up the audience with a sentimental song which she sings sitting on a garishly flower-decked swing. She then leaves the stage to Skinner, who dominates it, a man of justice, invoking the spirit of morality and respect for the rule of law:

Fellow Americans. How we run the law's the same how we live our lives. The store, street, law: one. Let the law slip: you git bad measure in the store and the sidewalk end up death row for the good citizen. That's how it is!

The sentenced victim is brought on stage. It is not Paul, the expected black victim, but Fred, who is very, very white. They tie him to the flowery swing, and Skinner begins to wind the audience up into righteous fervour, setting Fred swinging out over the front stalls. A clown toys with Fred, squirting him with a water pistol, but finally it is the clown who shoots the first real bullets into Fred. The audience then explodes into gunfire which continues for some minutes, while Fred twitches and jerks into death. The scene ends with his body pouring blood onto the stage while Skinner, "like a venerable senator", urges the audience into 'The Star-Spangled Banner'.

This, one of the most terrible acts of violence in Bond's work, shocks and moves so deeply because the whole weight of a society's morality has been mobilised to crush an innocent person publicly and proudly. It is not something that goes on in a corner, like the baby-stoning, or Lear's blinding. Neither can we comfortably judge Skinner for cynical cruelty. On the contrary, he is terrifyingly sincere. Apart from the skill with which it is constructed, the scene's most telling point is that the 'real' audience sit, presumably in awed silence, while their avenging counterparts (on tape in the first production) cheer, scream and empty their revolvers into Fred, so that complicity in the legal murder is shared, while the real audience observe and make their own judgement on what they see. By infecting the audience with some responsibility for the events, and confronting them with their own potential for socially-approved violence, the play generates anti-bodies against the more immediate plagues that threaten progressive ideas.

There is a coda to *The Swing* played out in the theatre the next morning. Stagehands are clearing up, a photographer snaps the body, and Paul comes on to be met by Ralph. Paul announces that he is leaving Mrs. Kroll's service, not in protest at Fred's slaughter, but because he's had an application in at the mine office for over a month. He shows no emotion at the previous night's events, but he can't afford to. He is a black man. The racist society which has slaughtered his friend has now absorbed him into its body as a worker. Ralph is set fair to continue his father's brutalised life, and the stage-hands squabble over a coin that Paul, in a gesture of disgust, tosses at them. *The Swing* is a play that offers no way out. The only moments of love and friendship, between Greta and Ralph, and between Paul and Fred are quickly smashed, and there are no new young people in this play to build a new society. America, after all, has not built the new society in which the human need to love and to learn are respected. One of Bond's most potent contributions to a theatre of politics, is that, by constantly cutting back to the social and economic basis of life as he does in *The Swing*, he reveals the source of our reactionary ways. He is not 'fair to both sides', as is sometimes said, because although few writers create such vivid, yet transparent reactionary characters, they are placed in social contexts which show how their corrupt ideas have been arrived at.

Bond is a socialist, personally convinced of the revolutionary potential of the working class in this country. His criticisms of Stalinist approaches to social change in *Lear* should not obscure his belief that revolution can be made successfully. Lear's violence certainly does make that of Cordelia almost inevitable, but our society, it is suggested, is different. The preconditions for successful revolution, not present in Lear's society, are there in ours. "Our revolution", writes Bond, "has to be made at a much higher stage of social, technological and economic organisation than any previous one. For it to work, the majority of people must become concerned and articulate about the nature of our society."

The creating and spreading of a critical awareness is, of course, an important job for the committed artist. That process is also helped along by the very nature of modern capitalism which relies heavily on advanced technology. As Bond analyses it, ". . . technology needs a certain level of enlightenment in order for it to run, and for consumers to exercise choice (however limited). Capitalism needs a liberal facade and therefore a number of liberal practices. It can never shut this hole in its defences." So, with this combination of raised consciousness and the contradictions inherent in modern capitalism, a revolution is possible, although not necessarily inevitable. It has to be worked for. "We have to destroy the image of man the primitive animal and replace it with the idea of socialist man, and the society, not merely of equal opportunity but of practical equality. I don't believe it would be possible to seize power by armed means till this is done."

Bond's plays are about the strengths, real and potential, of individuals in social situations. His politics insist that despite the compromises and failures, a commitment to human freedom must not be lost, that change is possible, that human beings can take control of their lives, that they are, finally, rational.

# 5:INTIMATES

It is through man's relationships with his intimates – family, friends, lovers – that the dominant ideology of society works, and it is these relationships which have usually formed the basic subject-matter of theatre. We are shaped by our families, but our families take their cue from the society in which they exist; so it is to be expected that a playwright like Bond, who wants to analyse society right back to its roots, will have important things to say about the family and about the other intimate relationships that are coloured by society's values.

Although the institution of the family is currently under attack from some quarters, it should be remembered that not all of the criticism has been of the family as such but rather of the particular function that the family has been required to perform in advanced capitalist countries, and of the corruption of loving relationships that has resulted. The attack has centred on the growing 'optimisation' of the family, not as the best arrangement for mutual love and support between adults, but into a unit of isolated consumption so that capitalism may run more 'efficiently'. The victims of this increasing isolation are particularly the old, the women and the children.

The more isolated, physically and spiritually, modern families become, and the better consumers they are, the more easily they can be induced to pass on the values of the consuming society to their children. The role of the family in Bond's plays is often to be just such a transmitter of cultural values. *Early Morning*, for example, uses the fluidity and freedom of dreams to show how the values we live by today were created, and how they are passed on. The play deals with families, and how the family and society become mirror-images of each other. Setting the play in a quasi-Victorian England, Bond shows how certain stereotypes of the Mother, Father, Brother and Lover become mythologised into an ideological system of ideas and superstitions. Bond was quoted in the New York Times as saying:

> I find it curious the way that an image can dominate whole groups of people and, when one looks at the same image a little later, it's very, very funny . . . I wanted to show how people are trapped by these myths and how they must shake them off if they're ever to be really free. [9]

The title *Early Morning* suggests that Victorian Britain was a kind of birth-time for a country and a culture now somewhere into its afternoon or late evening. Technology was beginning to offer a potentially liberating grasp on the environment, and it was important for control to be established more and more firmly. The way to do this without causing too much dissent was through that highly potent brew of ideology, religion and imagery which found its best expression in the semi-mythical figure of Victoria. By establishing the view that society, like the ideal family, should be disciplined, moral, dedicated to the hard work of trade and commerce, and above all authoritarian, and by transmitting that idea to children, society would, in theory, become more stable and controllable. Bill Gaskill, who commissioned and directed the first, illegal, performances of the play, once suggested that it had a three-part structure which showed Arthur's indoctrination into this mythical world, his reaction to it, and his escape from it. It is a vivid metaphorical description of what happens to most of us in some form or another.

According to this interpretation, Scenes 1 to 5 represent a kind of 'Childhood' for Arthur. He is surrounded by grotesque adults, figures of arbitrary authority, who rule the world in much the same way that parents rule the child's world. Albert feels threatened by his wife's power, and is plotting to kill her, and so he tries to enlist his son's support. There'll be no trouble with George, the other son, who is, in Bond's words, "the pure socialised version" of his brother. George can be relied upon to follow precedent and do as he's told, but Arthur, his unseparated Siamese twin, is a nuisance. He won't support Albert and his henchman Disraeli, but neither will he oppose them. A claustrophobic family power struggle is in progress here. Father and Mother fight for the child's affection, but the child, Arthur/ George, is two distinct people: George the Conformer, and Arthur the Rebel. Yet they cannot move without each other. The adult world is full of scheming and plotting, which Albert expresses in contemporary military/ historical terms: "It must look as if some stray fanatic kills her. We just step in to keep the peace. We close the ports and airfields, take over the power stations, broadcast light classics and declare martial law." (These anachronisms are important because they link the present with the past, showing them to be different variations of the same basic action.)

Albert represents his scheming to overthrow the Queen as the height of progressive thought, a new scientific, trading spirit ousting outdated absolute Royal power. What he in fact says shows that he has the same dominating and patronising attitude to the people that is the conservative norm for most adult relations with children: "The people are strong. They want to be *used* – to build empires and railways and factories, to trade and convert and establish law and order." Arthur, as a child in this adult world, is excluded from participating in adult affairs, and so his reaction is to opt out of society's apparently absurd goings-on. Unfortunately he can't, because he is joined to George who in turn is about to be joined, in wedlock, to Florence Nightingale. She is the establishment's archetype of correct femininity, a gentle nurse symbolically mopping the fevered brow of an Empire. (In Bond's unsentimental variation, the lady of the lamp also dispenses sexual relief to the Crimean war-wounded.) Arthur's unwilling involvement in society is fixed when, during the bungled assassination attempt, George, with whom he shares vital internal organs, is accidentally shot. The period of childhood, when children at are first denied responsibility, and then have it thrust upon them too late, is over.

Continuing this interpretation, Scenes 6 to 15 represent 'Adolescence'. They show Arthur drawn inexorably into the activity of a mad world. He hates it, but takes part in it because he has no choice. As George begins to die and to rot on his shoulder, Arthur finally decides to act; but like many adolescents, he can only see things in terms of the values that surround him.

All the plotting, killing and militarism is to him clear evidence of an inbuilt destructiveness, almost a death wish, in human beings. "Doctor", he says, "Hitler had vision. He knew we hated ourselves, and each other, so out of charity he let us kill and be killed." His answer to this awesome problem is a second Final Solution. He organises a grotesque tug-of-war on the cliffs of Beachy Head, in which the combined weight of both sides will cause a land-slip and kill everybody. This is social involvement of a sort, but it is based on the common prejudice that man is by nature doomed to be destructive and aggressive. By these lights, annihilation must seem sensible. Unfortunately, Arthur discovers his mistake when he reaches the foot of the cliff where lie the newly dead. He shoots himself (part of the plan), only to find that George appears as a ghost and re-attaches himself to his Siamese twin.

With the realisation that despair and suicide haven't changed the situation very much, 'Adulthood', the last phase (Scenes 17-21) begins. In heaven, life proceeds much as it did on earth. It is, though, a living death, and Arthur realises that it is no different from being alive: "Most people die before they reach their teens. Most die when they're still babies or little children. A few reach fourteen or fifteen. Hardly anyone lives on into their twenties . . . Souls die first and bodies live." Arthur, in this heaven, just doesn't fit in. It's almost as if there is something in him, a 'soul', or something quintessentially human, which has not died. Unsubdued even after his entire body has been eaten, Arthur survives: "I'm alive. Or I'm beginning to live." As he rises above his coffin in the final scene, he reaches a desperate kind of maturity. He even looks old, with long, uncombed hair and a beard. It is a humanistic resurrection. Griss pronounces an epitaph, which for Arthur, marks a real beginning: " 'E weren' a bad bloke. Juss couldn't keep 'is-self to 'is-self. Thass a fault – but it don' make yer wicked."

Full of a strange and beautiful grandeur, *Early Morning* is a liberating play theatrically, and yet, like many dreams, rooted in the day-to-day details of experience. By choosing a surrealist theatrical style to express dialectical arguments, Bond does more than make politics disconcertingly funny. He illuminates those politics by means of a style and an imagery which unite history, national politics, and the politics of the family and child development into one rich stage metaphor. Bond even admitted in the programme for *Narrow Road* at the Belgrade, that he had sympathy with those who saw *Early Morning* and didn't understand exactly what was happening: "I can sympathise with that, though it wasn't true of everybody. It goes through all I know about life and it was very difficult to get all that in one play."

*Early Morning* is typical of Bond's plays in that it admires child-like values. The idea of the child as symbol of hope and fulfilled human potential lies deep within most of his work. In families, children are the main target for the individualistic, competitive ideology that it is the family's job to transmit, and the education that takes place in most schools emphasises that this is normal. In fact, historical evidence suggests that in other cultures and in other times, children went through a very different kind of conditioning, one in which they were given real responsibility – as shepherds, perhaps, farmworkers or child-carers – simply out of the need to deploy every energy in order to survive.

The grotesque world of adults – the fluidity and
freedom of dreams used to illuminate cultural
history. The trial in *Early Morning,* Royal
Court Theatre, London 1968.
(Photo: Douglas Jeffery)

A statement of possibilities in a hostile world –
the final moments of *Saved.*
(Photo: Gerald Chapman)

With affluence, children are no longer needed commercially, except as consumers, and so they are not treated as slaves, but neither are they assumed to have much to contribute of their own creativity. That is surely what Arthur means when he claims that most people die before their teens, and that hardly anyone lives into their twenties. It is also the thought behind Bond's *The Death of Childen*, part of an introduction to his translation of Wedekind's *Spring Awakening*, which pinpoints the massive contradiction in the way we bring up children:

> The children are told that life has meaning and purpose, that their own actions count and so they must be careful what they do, that they must treat life as an adventure, and that they live in a democracy. But the children who go to the barrack schools in our cities know that they will pass dull lives (the excretory metaphor is intended) in grey, ugly cities, will only be able to show initiative when they strike, and will have no democratic responsibility for the future and welfare of even their own family.

So far, excepting *The Woman,* there are no children (other than babies) in Bond's stage plays. However, in the filmscript *Walkabout* (of all the films Bond has written, the one least easily dismissed) Bond does create a significant part for a child. A young boy, who is about eight or nine, and his teenage sister are driven out into the Australian outback by their father, who tries to murder them, and then kills himself. They are stranded in the desert, helped only by a young aborigine who is on his 'walkabout', the test of endurance and self-reliance that every aborigine youth goes through. The boy soon adapts to the ways of the desert, while his adolescent sister, who has spent far more time in a sterile middle-class education system, clings to her 'civilised' values which result in a death of despair for the young aborigine.

The image of the child, which can be embodied equally in adults and in old people (for instance in Lear: "I must become a child, hungry and stripped and shivering in blood . . .") holds out the possibility of new life and fresh starts. The child is important in Bond not because of his weakness but because of his strength. At the end of *We Come to the River*, the Old Woman sings to the Child:

> Shall I tell you who is strong?
> Child, you are strong
> You have nothing and your hands are small
> But the world spins like clay on a potter's wheel
> And you will shape it with your hands.

The characters in the plays who are really strong are not those who maintain a specious innocence, where that means ignorance. Wendla in *Spring Awakening* dies because of her innocence, and both Lear and Shakespeare build walls to protect themselves from knowledge.

The Son, in *Bingo*, ends up talking about the mythical land of space and freedom to which he will go: "Where no one stand 'tween me an' my god, no one listen when I raise the song a praise, an' I walk by god's side with curtsey an' fear nothin', as candid loike a child." His innocence is most dangerous because it is based on cheap metaphysics and ignorance. History suggests that his destination might well be the Americas, and his descendants the likes of Mr. Skinner in *The Swing*. The strong ones are rather those who are able to accept their experience as real, in spite of being told over and over again that it is not. Len in *Saved*, Arthur in *Early Morning* and the Dead people in the opera manage it, but at terrible cost to each of them. Lear recognises that he must become a child again to find strengths, and Willy and Rose (in *The Sea*) are both children in a rather mad and hostile world which takes away those closest to them, and leaves them with terrifying adult-figures like Hatch and Mrs. Rafi. Bond's central characters are all engaged in a similar search for the knowledgeable child and a struggle with the ignorant child in themselves.

At the other end of society are another group of people, the old, who are at great risk in the consuming society. Old people have a vital and important role to play in the historical societies Bond writes about. There is, of course, a conflict between the necessarily authoritarian tendency of assuming that wisdom resides solely in the old *because* they are old, and Bond's more anarchist position that wisdom is available to all, that it is not just experience but the way we interpret experience that matters. Sometimes the old have nothing to teach, or what they teach is dehumanising and reactionary. Alen (in *The Pope's Wedding*), Harry (in *Saved*), Lear before his downfall, Mrs. Rafi, Shakespeare, and Mr. Skinner all to some extent corrupt the young by what they teach. On the other hand Evens (who warns against trusting the wise old fool too much), Lear at the play's end, and even Harry, manage to pass on some clues for happiness to the young, even if the real message is simply the unspoken determination to make a relationship, as Harry does with Len.

The old will always be at risk in capitalist societies because they can no longer produce wealth, and while their children and grandchildren grow into tight, insular units, they find themselves isolated and unable to contribute even to their families, let alone society. Bond invests his old people with a dignity and poignancy which demonstrates what is lost as personal contact is eroded between grandparent and grandchild, teacher and pupil, craftsman and apprentice. The loss is both social, and personal. Mrs. Rafi's vision of herself old may be self-pitying, almost self-aggrandising, but without understanding the reasons, she graphically demonstrates the cold consequences of our way of treating human relationships:

> You give up shouting. You close your eyes and the tears dribble down your ugly old face and you can't even wipe it clean – they won't give you your hanky. 'Don't let her have it. She gets into a tizzy and tears it to shreds.' There you are: old, ugly, whimpering, dirty, pushed about on wheels and threatened. I can't love them. How could I? But that's a terrible state in which to move towards the end of your life: to have no love.

Mrs. Rafi is a victim of the taboos against tenderness built into the nervous system of our culture. It is in the corruption and destruction of the most intimate and tender human relationships that Bond shows up the wider corruption. Tenderness is not a quality that is opposed to the sensible, rational mind, nor is it even just a partner or a complement to rationality. Human tenderness for Bond is an *expression* of human rationality, a normal and even mundane part of living which nevertheless has constantly to be argued for, nurtured and protected because our social organisation is so hostile to it. The rationality of tenderness and love can be partly justified by the animal need to protect the young and hence the species, but in human beings, who make their own conscious choices, it has only to justify itself.


Tenderness can often be expressed sexually in Bond's plays. His writing about sexual relationships is as often focussed on the social meanings and use of sexuality as on its private pains and pleasures. In rigidly-controlled societies such as the Japan of Shogo and Georgina or the England of Lear or Victoria, the usefulness of sexual repression to a ruling class is relatively clear. Sexual and emotional freedom practised in private would be a continuing criticism of the lack of political freedom in wider society. (In this sense, a true democracy would be a social equivalent of individual tenderness). Laws did half the job, but not always successfully. It was guilt above all that these societies used to rein in personal freedoms, guilt transmitted primarily through the institutions of family and school. Georgina is typical of these agents of guilt, herself riven with it. The communicators of guilt, and often its most damaged victims, tend, in Bond's work, to be women. The recurrent pattern is that of a male-dominated society using women to fix in the young 'correct' ideas about sexual behaviour – women being, as mothers and infant teachers, traditionally the direct communicators of cultural values to the young and very young. Behind the corrupted tenderness of Bodice and Fontanelle lie the terrible errors of their father Lear, behind the crabbed sensitivity of Judith sits her father Shakespeare. Even Queen Victoria apes the male cultural patterns of her class and her ministers. But it is Georgina, in *Narrow Road*, who most clearly articulates her role as a transmitter of sexual guilt in the service of power politics:

> I persuade people in their hearts that they are sin, and that they have evil thoughts, and that they're greedy and violent and destructive, and – more than anything else – that their bodies must be hidden, and that sex is nasty and corrupting and must be secret. When they believe all that they do what they're told.

There is tragedy, after the absolute self-deception of this, in Georgina's sexually-disturbed madness, but there is at least a sense of justification, a feeling that she has drawn her fate on her own head. On the other hand, in *The Swing*, Greta's tragedy is so haunting because her human tenderness is so evident and her vulnerability in society so total. Prevented from openly enjoying her sexuality, she finds it furtively in Book Two of Virgil's *Aeneid*: "Aeneas' son saw the naked body. We covers ours _ like you put blemished fruit at the back of the store. Don't some of them wash? Ralph, have you – as your teacher – tell me – did you ever see a woman's breast?" As she reads on, she unbuttons her dress to uncover one of her breasts. "When the lady's breasts are firm it means she likes the man. Always remember. The sign of fondness. Now you've seen what Aeneas and his son saw." When the action changes with Paul's and Skinner's entrances, the two young people re-learn their guilt and both go mad. Greta may or may not have been touched on the breast in the dark, but whatever happened seriously disturbs her. She becomes obsessive and disoriented. Ralph's madness, on the other hand, wears the same clothes as that of the society that he lives in, and is therefore well camouflaged. It results in the obsessive righteousness with which he joins in the execution of Fred. It is, of course, highly probable that it was he, having once been denied the chance, who touched Greta in the dark.

The taboos on tenderness throughout Bond's work which damage men and women alike are part of the distorted sexual environment created by male- and class-dominated society. Bond's portrait of Patty in *The Fool* shows just what strength is needed to survive as a working-class woman in such a society. She is married to a poet who is a labouring peasant, an object amongst the gentry of patronising enthusiasm. He can't earn a living, however, and so the real burden of supporting their family falls heavily on her. That family is trapped from the outset in an economic vice. Clare's need to write is as real and as normal as his need for love: "Can't help what I am. God knows I wish I couldn't write me name! But my mind git full a songs an' I on't feel like a man if I on't write 'em down." But Patty's realities are of another order from her husband's: "One kid on my hands an' another on the way. Tired a all this self. You think a someone else. Feed *us*. Thass your job boy . . . Aches an' pains? I'll know what smartin' is when I hev your kid."

The tortured relationship between Patty and Clare is made more complex by his love for Mary. They only met once, but Mary henceforward haunts him with her promise of a free, independent life. It is, of course, a sentimental promise because for all Clare's dreams about living in the forest with her, the reality is that Mary has been thrown out of her job and has joined the gypsies. She can't marry Clare because she is effectively an outlaw, but she can find some satisfaction, even laughs, in going with the travellers. Clare, however, can't let her image go, and as he becomes more mad, so her memory becomes more real to him. He begins to talk of her as his "real wife", so adding more weight to Patty's burden. Under such emotional and material pressure, it is not to be wondered at that she becomes bitter and despairing. However her view of him as a "scribbler" who refuses to get work does not make her the philistine nagger whose need for new shoes, a shirt, a "bit a ribboned", and a decent meal is frivolous beside those of her poet husband. It is only the rich like Mrs. Emmerson who think that they should support Clare no matter what: "If only you surround him with assurance and support. Surely he can find peace in this garden?" In the end, the rights to both a sufficient physical and cultural life, made to clash in Patty and Clare, are not divisible. When Clare's society attempts to divide them, it drives him mad, and it brings great misery to Patty. Her final appearance is one of Bond's most moving affirmations of human strength, such that, for the first time, a woman character comes near to being the centre of the play. This strength is, however, one for which she has had to pay dearly. Both her children have died, and she has survived as best she can. Her final words to Clare define the common-place courage that women of her class were forced to find, and the numbness that must come in its wake: "Sorry you on't had a proper life. Us hev t' make the most of what there is. On't us boy? No use lettin' goo. Learn some way t' stay on top. I'd be a fool t' cry now. 'Bye 'bye."

*Saved* draws together a web of all these kinds of intimate relationships to show how people survive emotionally in a world which seems to have no place for them. Both family relationships and sexual ones in *Saved* have deteriorated into cold hostility and aggression.

The history and work experience of her family show that despite so-called social progress, people like Pam are subject to pressures as intimidating as, if more dangerously subtle than, those on Patty. Just as in *The Pope's Wedding*, work is the ever-present but understated backdrop to all relationships. "'Ow's the job?" asks Fred. "Stinks," says Len. "It don't change", says Fred, and in that kind of etched exchange, a whole world of experience is fixed. When Harry interrupts Len and Pam on the family sofa, he is getting ready for work. There is no clear indication of time, but Len is toying with the idea of staying the night with Pam, so it seems to be evening at least, and Harry is probably off on night shift. He appears to go out at about the time that Mary is expected back in, so that their work patterns reinforce their already antagonistic relationship. Len even has to ask Pam if she lives alone, as if her parents do not exist. In Scene Two, she elaborates a little on her family. Len has moved in as a lodger, and he asks her if her mother minds their relation-ship. "Don't have to", says Pam, "Your money comes in 'andy." Twice when Len asks her about her parents, Pam answers "Never arst . . . never listen." Her family is obviously an irritant to her, but Len persists in nosing out her history:

LEN. Must a bin bloody rotten when yer was a kid.
PAM. Never know'd no difference. They 'ad a boy in the war.

That last revelation, and the fact that he was killed by a bomb in a park suddenly show the closed world of the family in historical perspective. Just like this child, Pam's baby too is killed in a park, a place supposedly of recreation, safety and joy. Whether it comes about through bombs dropped by enemy airmen, or stones thrown by hooligans, the avoidable deaths of the two babies leave wounds in other people which eventually turn to numbness. The accumulation of everyday horror, of which bombing was just the most public, leaves the family blighted. "She never mentions 'im an' 'e never mentions 'er." Finally Len, with his tactless but caring curiosity, remarks "I never got yer placed till I saw yer ol' people", and Pam, almost as if acknowledging, against her will, that she *does* carry something of her parents, explodes "I never chose 'em." Len's arrival begins to change the family. By Scene Four, he seems to be a substitute son, fed and cared for by Mary, even though Pam has tired of him and wants him out of the house. By Scene Nine, Len and Mary's sexual frustration nearly turns them into Oedipal lovers, and in Scene Twelve, after the terrible row between Mary and Harry about that sexually explosive incident, Len and Harry manage to make a relationship, however tentative. "Thought yer might like someone t' say goodnight." says Harry, in a moment as crucial as any in the whole of this play. It's as if Len, by part-seducing Mary, manages to gain a small toe-hold in the family, and Harry, despite his outraged propriety, understands this.

Children and women are both subject to insult and casual hatred in *Saved* because they have no status in the hard, angry society in which they live. The urge to act 'grown-up', to be aggressive, competitive and generally insensitive results in things to do with childhood constantly being put down. Len's judgement on Fred, " 'E's gone back like a kid", and Pam's on Len, "You're juss like a kid", indicate what value a child has. Only Pam has another perspective: "Yer wouldn't 'elp a cryin' baby!", but Pam is also one of the four people in Scene Four who ignore a crying baby, an act of violence which seems almost as culpable as the murder, because the baby is conscious and because there is an expectation that a family will care. Mary, Pam and Len all shrug off responsibility for the child on to another member of the family. Even Len reckons "It'll cry itself t'sleep." One solution to the baby's problem is to "put it on the council", and another, sown in Pam's mind in this scene, is to give it aspirins. Len's loyalty to the kid and to Pam are all very well, but like Basho, he still leaves a child to its own devices. The scene ends with the baby sobbing away into silence.

The tenderness which is missing in the family is hardly likely to be present in the older children of this society either, and the gang in Scene Six treat sex as both mucky and unattainable. Their taunting of Mary, when Len goes over to her, is aggressive and desperately insecure "One man's meat . . . more like scrag-end . . . Bit past it aint she? . . . She's still got the regulation 'oles . . ." and so on. Even the moment when they decide to "enjoy themselves" with the baby has the ring of erotic guilt about it.

MIKE (*quietly*). Reckon it's all right?

COLIN (*quietly*). No one around . . .

PETE (*quietly*). Yer can do what yer like.

BARRY. Might as well enjoy ourselves.

PETE (*quietly*). Yer don't get a chance like this everyday.

Women, for these lads, are the prey they go hunting for in the church youth club and the all-night laundries. At the same time, they see themselves as the prey of women. "There's plenty a blokes knockin' about. Why don't yer pick on someone else," Mike says. "Yer can 'ave me, darlin'. But yer'll 'ave t' learn a bit more respect." Whereas the women just about hold their own against the men in *The Pope's Wedding*, both men and women in *Saved* are victims of the sexual double standard. Sexual drive is mixed with fear and loathing of women, who are associated with the equally dreaded fates of venereal disease and babies.

*Saved* shows the erosion of a family under social pressures – war, work alienation, sexual frustration, despair – and the beginning of re-integration through Len's slow and unostentatious determination to cling to his humanity. The final, almost wordless scene, presents a remarkably full picture of the new stage reached by the family. Some kind of equilibrium has been achieved. Mary, despite her earlier threat to keep herself to herself, has returned to her cooking and cleaning duties. Pam just sits and reads Radio Times. Harry quietly, almost religiously, does his pools, as if writing to God. Len mends the chair broken in the row. It is peace, but it is a barren peace. Only Len, the mender, speaks, and no-one answers his request to "Fetch me 'ammer." His chair-mending is healing, but the other elements in the stage-picture show that it can never be enough. The play concludes in what Bond calls "a silent social stalemate," after having established, through Len, the truly astonishing potential for an unsentimental and wholly human love. It also shows that such love growing in a dehumanised culture is, at best, only a statement of possibilities.

# 6:THE INDIVIDUAL AND ART

(Man) is not satisfied with being a separate individual; out of the partiality of his individual life he strives towards a 'fullness' that he senses and demands, towards a fullness of life of which individuality with all its limitations cheats him, towards a more comprehensible, a more just world, a world, that *makes sense.*

Ernst Fischer, The Necessity of Art

Characters frequently go mad in Bond's plays. Georgina, Hatch, Clare, Greta are all destined to end up in mental institutions in the grip of their own daft fantasies. Kiro and Shakespeare may not be clinically certifiable, but they both commit suicide in moments of acute despair. Lear and Arthur both go through a time of extreme mental torment from which they emerge with the beginnings of a new sanity. The final stage picture of *We Come to the River* offers a bleak image of the world, one divided between sane but dead victims and living but mad inmates of an asylum. These kinds of overt madness in Bond's work occur when there is some violent rupture between the reality inside an individual, and the social reality he or she lives by. Georgina, for instance, goes mad because her faith in God and Man are simultaneously destroyed by the soldiers who kill the children she is caring for. Hatch, in *The Sea*, invests his life, not in God, but in small time capitalism and, as that is destroyed by Mrs. Rafi, his sense of oppression is diverted to mythical creatures from outer space. Clare, Shakespeare and Kiro likewise find that they have committed themselves wholly to absurdities, and the disappointment and shock of discovering the truth make them go mad. These are reasonably well-defined madnesses, but there are other sorts in Bond.

R. D. Laing writes that 'the condition of alienation, of being asleep, of being unconscious, of being out of one's mind, is the condition of the normal man', and that is the state in which many of the survivors of Bond's plays find themselves. Cordelia and her ministers are mad, according to Lear, because they have no pity, "and the man without pity is mad". The mad heaven of *Early Morning*, where mutual cannibalism is the norm, is infected by what Queen Victoria calls Arthur's "lunacy", but her kind of normality, identified with polite, ordered, static societies, turns out to be vicious and cruel, despite the rhetoric of common sense it claims to live by. It proves too to be deeply irrational. The world of *The Swing* is just such normality, as is the post-revolutionary kingdom ruled over by what Lear describes as "good, decent, honest, upright lawful men who believe in order." "I have lived with murderers and thugs," he tells the Old Councillor, "there are limits to their greed and violence, but you decent, honest men devour the earth!" The economic, social and moral values of these societies clash violently with the essentially human pressure to be happy and sane and so the plays become battlegrounds between sanity-seeking individuals and corrupt cultures.

*Bingo* deals with different kinds of individual madness, and with the failure of an individual to oppose corruption in his own life, thus inviting madness. With characteristic irony, it is the Old Man (who has, his wife tells Shakespeare, "the mind of a twelve year ol' an the needs on a man") who probably comes closest to fulfilling his human potential. He is, after all, the only person who takes care of the Young Woman after she has been whipped for being a vagrant. Shakespeare does offer her first clothes and then money; but when Combe, the landowner with whom he is doing business, sets to to have her recaptured, Shakespeare just complains irritably about the disturbance to his peace and quiet. Judith's ungenerous propriety is outraged by the girl who is, to her, "dirty" in all senses. But then, she has been ground down by her father's self-absorption and the isolation to which he has unthinkingly condemned her. The Old Man is literally the victim of a violent culture, accidentally rendered subnormal by the blunt side of a fellow soldier's axe as he was chopping up a fallen enemy. His childlike nature is a sad burden for his wife, who also has to 'mother' Shakespeare, but there is in his enforced simplicity a new innocence. He plays in the snow like a child, he has to be given "a nice surprise" when he's upset, and he behaves with that attractive purity of emotional response of many mentally-handicapped people. When he realises that the Young Girl will be hanged, his mind fills with the images and sights of the hanging and he cries at their obscenity: "O dear, I do hate a hanging. People runnin' through the streets laughin an' sportin'. Buyin' an' sellin'. I allus enjoyed the hangings when I were a boy. Now I can't abide 'em." He is a simpleton, like King Lear's Fool, and that gives him a kind of abnormal critical power, but it is limited and ineffective, precisely because he is not 'normal'. As Judith points out, he has "no responsibilities, no duties". Society, run by men like Combe and Shakespeare, excludes him. When he is accidentally shot dead by his own son, reality, crude and violent, muscles its way into other-worldliness.

The Old Man's son represents another kind of madness, and another of Bond's ironic but well-justified conjunctions of different impulses. On the one hand, he is obsessively religious in a puritanical, fundamentalist way. On the other, he has an acute sense of injustice, so much so that he becomes the leader of the local peasantry as they fill in the ditches dug to mark out enclosed common land. The two impulses become inextricably bound together, of course, and his vision of a just world, where rich thieves won't plunder the common land shades imperceptibly into a vision of paradise: "I looked across a great plain into his eyes. A sword were put into my yand. The lord god a peace arm us. We must go back an' fill up they ditches agin t' night." The Old Man says of his son: "He rage up an' down all hours . . . He 's allus talkin' t' god – so stands t' reason he never listen to a word I say", and indeed the young man seems to be close to hysteria much of the time. Nevertheless his real madness is exposed in his lack of human sympathy. Looking at the gibbetted body of the Young Woman, he observes: "Death bring out her true life, brother. Look, her eyes be shut agin the truth. There's blood trickle down the corner a her mouth. Her teeth snap at her flesh while her die." His final decision to go away "where no one stand 'tween me an' my god, no one listen when I raise the song a praise" fits in which his religious obsession, but it is also a kind of self-imposed autism, another out-break of Scopey's disease.

Shakespeare's despair is also a kind of madness. His work is the evidence that he was under no crippling illusions about human nature, but he loses control because he won't carry his insights into his day-to-day life. His refusal to oppose the enclosures is a public sell-out to his own financial security, but his final despair is brought on by the decaying of his close personal relationships. He makes no significant attempt to protect the Young Woman from yet another whipping or from hanging, and Judith's reproaches seem quite justified: "You sit there and brood all day . . . I feel guilty if I dare to talk about anything that matters. I should shut up now – or ask if it's good gardening weather." Shakespeare's arrogant counter to this is: "You speak so badly. Such banalities. So stale and ugly." When his human responses have been so alienated that Judith's desperate complaints are heard only for their literary, or worse, their nuisance value, some vital moral connection in Shakespeare has clearly been broken. Bond's point is that if he had been stupid, he could be understood, if not excused, as an ageing reactionary. But Shakespeare was far from stupid, and Bond shows him monitoring his own alienation and self-hate all the way to suicide. He has, like Bond's Cordelia, an acute sense of justice, which is not so much reduced as institutionalised (in his case in his art, in hers in political ideology) and removed from any contact with life. And all the time, being Shakespeare, he observes the truth but does nothing to fight his despair:

I spent so much of my youth, my best energy . . . for this: New Place. Somewhere to be sane in. It was all a mistake. There's a taste of bitterness in my mouth . . . I howled when they suffered, but they were whipped and hanged so that I could be free.

Judith Shakespeare doesn't go mad, but her human responses are so ground down at the end of the play by her loveless existence in Shakespeare's house that she might just as well be. Her desperate scrabbling for a will as her father lies poisoned is heartless and unnatural, but it is, after all, perfectly attuned to her culture. Judith is another of Bond's damaged survivors, like Patty. While Shakespeare expires in self-disgust, she, because it is expected of women that they will always support and seldom be supported, remains at her post, supremely practical, tearing the bedroom apart for the money that will allow her and her mother to survive. But just as surely as Shakespeare dies, something human has died in Judith, too.

*Bingo* is a statement that, however terrible the pressures, it is necessary to live as close to the truth of one's own experience as possible. When that truth conflicts with the standards of the culture we live in, then an act of individual rebellion is called for. That individual action doesn't conflict with the need to act collectively in the cause of social change, because action, as opposed to religious self-purification of the kind that Basho went in for, involves other people. Shakespeare had the individual choice whether to oppose enclosure or not, but his decision not to made him part of the landowners' collective. If he had opposed it and joined the peasants' collective, he might have healed the broken connection between his sense of justice as a writer and as a man, and he would have had less reason to kill himself.

*The Fool* takes the dialectic between individual and collective sanity still further to show how the accumulated weight of a culture, its history, belief and social mores, press on and distort the individual personality. The idea of culture is of great importance to Bond. It signifies both the character of a society, its ideas and values, and its artistic expression. In his introduction to *The Fool*, he talks about the interwoven relationship between individual human nature and social culture:

> We don't have a fixed nature the way other animals do. We have a 'gap' left by our freedom from the captive nature of other animals, from the tight control of instincts. The gap is filled by culture. Human nature is, in fact, human culture.

That last idea makes the decisive link with Bond's ideas about religion and politics because if human nature *is* provisional, if it can be altered according to choice or circumstance, if we, and not some supernatural being, are solely responsible for our fates, then we have a responsibility to change society so that we can change ourselves. That is a responsibility which Shakespeare evaded.

One deadly enemy of a unified, healthy culture is class. In *The Fool* Bond shows how a developing middle-class culture, the first shoots of modern capitalism, begin to whittle away at the living working-class culture that had been able to survive under feudalism. On a winter's evening, a group of Mummers come to act out their traditional St. George and the Dragon play for their master, Lord Milton, and his guests. When their play has finished, both the Parson and Lord Milton use the occasion to lecture their workers on the need for pay restraint. It is an act symbolic of the changing nature of master/man relationships, and, parallel with this appropriation of the workers' cultural occasion, there goes a robbery by enclosure and drainage of the common land which has always provided a minimal independence for the rural working class. This theft of land has immediate repercussions in the farm-workers' riot. (There was in fact a wave of these food and enclosure riots in the nineteenth century. Bond's historical model is the rioting at Littleport in Cambridgeshire. Several rioters were hung at Ely, and a plaque is to be seen still over the porch in Ely Parish Church showing where the bodies were dumped overnight before burial.) The result of the riots is death and deportation for the farmworkers, but the results of the loss of their culture are more fundamental and widespread, and they find expression in the fate of John Clare. In the condemned cell at Ely prison, the men who performed plays for their master at Christmas-time are visited by Clare and Patty. In their conversation, Patty tells her sister Darkie that John's "scribblin' come t' summat. Gen'man bin. Talk 'bout a book." Miles asks him, "What you write boy? Write 'bout this place. What goo on", but Clare's answer "Who'd read that?" is an onimous forecast of his later predicament.

Walking in Hyde Park with his patroness Mrs. Emmerson, the working-class poet is shown to have been taken up as a fad by precisely that class

Two mad victims of a violent culture throw snowballs at each other. The Old Man and Shakespeare in *Bingo*, Northcott Theatre, Exeter, 1973.
(Photo: Nicholas Toyne)

The fate of the artist in bourgeois society: Mrs. Emmerson awaits John Clare's 'effusions'. *The Fool*, Royal Court Theatre, 1977.
(Photo: Chris Davies)

which was destroying the economic base on which he depended for a living. Mrs. Emmerson's very silly notion of Clare the poet is as someone inspired to soar on wings of verse by grass and trees: "It is my ambition to be at your side when the muse calls. I shall take down your words as you cast them on the air." The Admiral, who provides the financial muscle for Mrs. Emmerson's philanthropy, approves condescendingly of Clare's poetry: "Great charm there. True melody. Fine love of English landscape." But there are things he doesn't like: "I have one reservation. Not serious. The fault of a narrow horizon. Those remarks in – poem named after your village – which criticizes the landowning classes – smack of radicalism." The pressure on Clare, financial and political, begins to build. Mrs. Emmerson asks Clare naively: "How does it help to shake your fist at heaven when some homeward-wending swain perishes in the snow?" and Clare's brusque reply, "They had a winter coat they on't perish", suggests the growing gulf between the work Clare's rich London readership want from him and his own creative drive. In Scene Six that gulf has led to the beginnings of his madness, to bitter resentment from Patty, and to a state of near-starvation for the whole family. "On't goo back labourin'," Clare tells his wife. "On't know what I'm at out in the fields. Goo sit back the hedge an' write on me hat." For Mrs. Emmerson, Clare's art is decoration, and for Patty it is the fatal scribbling which stops him doing proper work and bringing wages in, but for Clare it is the only activity which it makes any sense for him to do: "Can't help what I am. God know I wish I couldn't write me name! But my mind git full a songs an I on't feel a man if I on't write 'em down."

As guilt about his family increases, as polite society begins to reject his poetry with its occasional radicalism and its dialect words, Clare sinks into illness and fantasies. He believes himself to be a boxer like those he saw in Hyde Park while Mrs. Emmerson was hovering in expectation of an "effusion". The black man and the Irishman, traditional victims of English exploitation, were able to earn money by knocking each other senseless for polite people to bet on, so why shouldn't he?: "Us'll hev t' git a proper job. Somethin' drastic t' bring in proper money. Set up boxin'. They git paid for bein' knocked about. I git knock about. Why on't I paid for it?" Clare realises that his culture's highest values are money-values, and he gives in to them; but capitulation takes his mind with it. In the asylum, Lord Milton and Clare, each wrapped in his own sense of failure, together locate the changes that have occurred in their culture. Clare sits in a bathchair, "a shrivelled puppet", mumbling, and Milton talks about the changes in the village, about his wife's death, about his son "in love with his factories." Clare is the inhabitant of the asylum, but the dislocations in Milton's, and Patty's life, remind us of his cry of outraged common sense just before being taken away in a straitjacket: "Hev the world gone mad? No wonder they say I'm a clown!"

In 1966, for the opening of a Royal Court production of *A Chaste Maid in Cheapside*, Edward Bond wrote a piece for The Guardian that defined his ideas about the symbiotic relationship of artist and society by looking at Thomas Middleton. Bond described him as "a hack". "His contemporaries did not think much of him", wrote Bond. "Jonson called him 'a base fellow', and he probably did not think much of himself as a writer . . . His writing was often lazy and conventional. Even his masterpiece is only partly his and partly that of a collaborator. He is of course hardly ever performed. He is probably the greatest English playwright after Shakespeare." [21] Bond sorts out that paradox by looking at the differences between Middleton's culture and our own. In our day, Bond suggests, a Thomas Middleton would be writing episodes of 'The Sweeney' or 'Z Cars'. However, violent and uncivilised as Middleton's society obviously was "it did allow, and *wanted*, its popular entertainers to probe deeply into human experience and the social order . . . Most writers can never by themselves be more than second-rate. Middleton's society made him first-rate. Ours makes most of its writers third-rate." [21]

That piece was written just three months after the critical hysteria over *Saved*, and it clearly shows Bond continuing a polemic with the society which had attempted first to neuter and then to kill his own play. Bond's pre-occupation with writers and their social role is not, however, mere gazing at his own professional navel. Art and imagination may be the tools of his trade, but they are also in many ways the life-blood of a culture. The creative need in aspiring professionals like Clare, or in people like the Mummers who create art because it is an integral part of community life, is one of the most characteristic human attributes. "Art", writes Bond in the introduction to *The Fool*, "is a direct record of the creation of human nature. It places the individual in the world, and interprets the world in accordance with possibilities and human needs. It expresses the real within the limits of knowledge at a particular time and in this way it has always been rational, even when this meant dancing for the rain."

This reference to magic suggests another mode in which art works. It implies power. When cavemen painted pictures of a hunting success, that symbol generated confidence which, in turn, created success in the next hunt. The 'magic' worked. Magic was augmented by tools, which were the means to make nature submit to man's wishes, and from that first tool-making creativity grew other forms which enabled man to understand and control ideas and feelings, as well as nature.

Today, art no longer holds a central position in society, except as a palliative or diversion, whose effect, conscious or otherwise, is to soothe discontent and discourage critical thinking. The fact that art now exists as either a part of the consumer leisure industry or as an embattled fringe activity critical of society as a whole, is more than just a shame. It is evidence of a dangerous internal flaw in society.

In *The Sea* Bond uses Mrs. Rafi to show how creativity can be subverted and misused, and to demonstrate the social consequences of that misuse. After Colin's death, the joint griefs of Willy and Rose are a social embarrassment because they cause questions to be asked which reflect on the town. To divert that potential criticism, the death is sentimentalised and its meaning denied by the dishonest ceremonial of a bankrupt Christian morality. The ceremony bids fair to be impressive enough, with its heavily-embroidered church banner

and fine-tuned hymns. But those hymns turn out to be the battleground over
which Mrs. Rafi and Mrs. Tilehouse struggle for power, the vicar's sermon is
full of a simplistic symbolism which obscures the real effect of Colin's death
on those close to him, and Mrs. Rafi's absurd encomium on Colin is a parody
of Victorian tragic verse, whose laboured couplets enfeeble any pretension to
gravity or sorrow:

Men who live out their little year
Are diamonds polished by their labours here
Fire has burned! It gives no ashes grey!
Diamonds only from this mortal clay!

The whole scenario, so carefully prepared by Mrs. Rafi is rendered overtly
ridiculous by Mrs. Tilehouse's rebellion, and by Hatch's entrance.

The whole funeral scene criticises the use of art and imagination to smother
thought, to mystify reality, and so evade responsibility for the life of the
community. Written and directed by Mrs. Rafi, the scene is part of a socially-
correct death-rhythm opposed to the struggling life-rhythm of the growing
consciousness within Willy and Rose. Mrs. Rafi's taste for grotesque celebra-
tions of death is made still more explicit in Scene Four, which shows
rehearsals for an entertainment to raise money for the coastguard including
the unhappy figure of mad Hatch. The occasion will, by this irony, at best
reinforce the tendency to self-destruction in the town, by maintaining Hatch
in a position of influence. In the same way that Hatch's appearance on the
clifftop undermines the pretensions of the funeral, so Rose, although grief-
stricken and struggling to find some way to comprehend her loss, criticises by
her very presence everything that takes place in the rehearsal room. Mrs.
Rafi works away attempting to divert attention from the embarrassing tragic
centre of Rose. The curtains are drawn, against Rose's wishes, so that she
will be kept from the sight of the sea. Bond studs the actual rehearsal with
jokes and comic business which demonstrate the absurdity and lack of
credibility of the art. Mrs. Rafi dominates everything and everyone. It's clear
that the performance is for her gratification alone, and the others have to find
their satisfaction within her structure. When Willy enters, his presence,
complementing Rose's, is used by Mrs. Rafi to spur what she calls their
"creativity" (in fact the opposite – the cheap exploitation of old cultural
conditioning). Mrs. Rafi as Eurydice is about to cross the Styx "made from
the tears of the penitent and suffering, which is interesting", and the nicely
comic bathos of that last clause locates for us the level at which Mrs. Rafi's
art deals with tears and suffering. When Jilly bursts into tears, moved by Mrs.
Rafi's rendering of the bizarrely-clichéd lines, "Eurydice, let me clasp your
marble bosom to my panting breast and warm it with my heart," she does so
in the presence of Willy and Rose, who have real cause to weep. After Jilly
has been dispatched with a servant for some comforting tea and cake, Mrs.
Rafi bashes on with her rehearsal, still imagining that she is uniquely close to
the heart of things and Jilly is simply hysterical: "Never mind books now
Vicar. We're struggling with life."

In the character of Hatch, Bond embodies an important irony. He is, in
Mrs. Rafi's words "over-imaginative for a draper", and he reckons himself
"more in the creative line". But however appropriate these statements might
be (and Hatch's invention of creatures from space who come down in airships

to take people's brains out deserves some kind of recognition!), the maturity of his imagination is plainly stunted. Hatch, oppressed by Mrs. Rafi and repressed by himself, invents a fantasy of revenge and aggression which enslaves both himself and men like Hollarcut. His imagination has been etiolated and made eccentric by the social stratification in the town, and by myths of social class and wealth. Even Mrs. Rafi is touched by these myths, but she can see no way out of them: "I'm tired of being a sideshow in their little world. Nothing else was open to me . . . Of course I have my theatricals." Her theatricals, and Hatch's fantasies, actually grow out of the same alienated world.

With these two characters Bond is drawing a most important distinction between fantasy on the one hand – the false inner world which people create when they have lost touch with reality – and, on the other hand, imagination. The imagination, and its denial, is what Bond's work is about, not because he sometimes writes about writers, but because the failure of his characters fully to realise their humanity is the result of a failure of imagination, which then leads on to a moral or a mental collapse. Imagination is our most essentially human faculty, because it allows us to predict the results of our actions, to see the connection between cause and effect. It thus has a vital moral dimension. A sense of responsibility is the result of a cultivated imagination, and a society which devalues the imagination, or which allows it to develop in children in the wrong way, will have a greatly diminished sense of morality. That is the basis of reasoning on which, I believe, Bond's moral force as a playwright rests, and these are the ideas which, as well as underpinning his arguments about the importance of art in a culture, are given vivid theatrical expression in the plays.


Thoughtlessness and cruelty, Bond shows, come about not because human beings are by nature thoughtless or cruel, but because their capacity for sympathy, their ability to *imagine* the feelings and the suffering of others, has been restricted and withered by the culture they live in. Given a culture where fantasies of aggression and the conservative ethic of individualism, competition and emotional self-sufficiency are transmitted at every level – in the home, at school, at work, in art, in political debate – it is hardly surprising that it will produce a Peter, who in Scene Three of *Saved,* attempts to elevate his running-down of a child in the road into a fantasy of deliberate child-killing. His mates support his bravado with their own defensive jokes, but Barry isn't convinced that Pete acted deliberately. The others kid him, and he has to retrieve his status by claiming: "I done blokes in . . . More'n you 'ad 'ot dinners. In the jungle. Shootin' up the yeller-niggers. An' cut 'em up after with the ol' pig-sticker." This, too, may be just a fantasy, but Barry *could* have seen Army service abroad in any one of a number of guerilla wars. Either way, violence and, later, sexual hatred expressed in jokes are the tools in the culture with which its members have to hack out some foothold of status and self-regard for themselves. What then takes place in Scene Six is a logical extension of this dehumanising process. Len and Fred talk about Pam while they fish, but they make no effort to imagine her feelings. "I thought she was goin' spare," says Fred, as if she were a chair.

When Pam arrives with her baby to spoil Fred's pleasures with her demands, she is on some kind of pills, presumably tranquillisers, and she has also given aspirin to the child to get some peace from the crying which she cannot understand. When the baby and the young men are eventually left together, the combination is ominous. The baby has been drugged into senselessness, and so cannot trigger any protective instincts in the young men, who are themselves drugged by a culture which values aggression before tenderness. As their treatment of the baby escalates from mild teasing to spitting, punching and hair-pulling, the values of that culture surface in their words

> COLIN. . ... Mind yer don't 'urt it.
>
> MIKE. Yer can't.
>
> BARRY. Not at that age.
>
> MIKE. Course yer can't, no feelin's.
>
> PETE. Like animals . . . Cloutin's good for 'em. I read it . . . Yer got a do yer duty.

Similar words were very probably spoken at Fred's trial.

There are other symptoms of anaesthetised imagination throughout the plays – for example in the Fourth Prisoner's blinding of Lear as a diplomatic manoeuvre to bring himself to the authorities' notice. The death of imagination and its replacement by fantasy conspire to destroy the human values of society; it is a process which Bond sees happening today, especially as technology grows more powerful. To fight these plagues, he finds antidotes only in a fully democratic, classless politics and the vigorous cultivation of creative imagination, whether in art, technology, politics or education. Bond is an artist, someone who makes professional use of his creative imagination: art is therefore his main weapon in this struggle. In the programme note to *We Come To The River*, composer and librettist together write:

> But art isn't about itself, it's about how men relate to the world and each other; it's not a private or even individual experience, but one of the ways society creates its identity; it's not primitive and dark, but rational and constructive.

Because Bond's art has radical social change as a conscious goal, his art (and perhaps all art) is inseparable from politics:

> Asking artists to keep politics out of art is as sensible as asking men to keep politics out of society. Men without politics would be animals, and art without politics would be trivial.

# 7:STAGECRAFT

I do consciously write for people who *behave* on the stage. When I write
a part for Shakespeare, I do have in a certain sense the technique of
someone like Frankie Howerd in mind.

Edward Bond

At least part of the reason for Bond's uneasy reputation has been the
problem of finding the right acting and staging style for his plays. Actors,
designers, directors and lighting artists are set special challenges by him,
although they are not challenges unique to this writer. In this chapter I want
briefly to look at the sort of theatre-writer Bond is technically, at some of the
effects he works for in performance and so try to elucidate helpful ground-
rules for performing his work.

The relationship that Bond aims for between performer and audience is
one in which the audience is an equal partner in the unfolding event. His
references to music-hall, and to seeing Frankie Howerd perform, suggest the
quality he is after:

If you go back to Frankie Howerd, the extraordinary thing was, one
realised in a sense one was performing a dance with him. You weren't
sitting there listening, he was reacting to you all the time. You knew what
the climax was, he knew what the climax was, but you worked together
for it.

This idea of partnership is particularly suited to Bond's plays because they
invariably have a learning momentum, and the audience is implicated in the
learning process along with the central characters. The sharing of a process of
discovery implies a wider, political idea about the writer's relationship with
his audiences:

I think the difference between the artist and the audience is very little. The
artist has a technical skill, that's all. But the audience is as 'profound',
'inspired' and what have you. Creativity is a common quality . . . Just to
use your five senses and your intelligence to orientate yourself through life
and to earn your living: these are creative actions.

Bond's plays show social processes in action, so his characterisation is
firmly rooted in particular classes and societies. The actor has, therefore, to
contact his audience primarily through the social detail and political facts that
Bond offers. This is not to say that all character is reducible to some stereo-
typed class role or function, only that no characters exist apart from society
and social pressures. (If they do, they end up in real or metaphorical
asylums.) Actors have the advantage that Bond establishes, with remarkable
speed and economy, precise social detail, even for quite minor figures. In a
large cast play like *Lear*, where a whole society is shown in cross-section,

workmen, soldiers and prisoners who are identified in the script only by a letter or a number are nevertheless given social identities, usually by their accent and their language. More important characters are given a rich social background on which the actor can work. In *The Swing,* for instance, Mrs. Kroll's life as a vaudeville artist, and her relationship with the town, is carefully woven into the scenes. Her daughter Greta expresses one set of reference points: "Our situation is unique. We live on the border between civilisation and barbarism. Which way shall we go? Do we know the answer?", and Skinner another: "This town's gonna boom. The company's stipulatin' for three hundred more miners next year. An families." In between those two views of society, Mrs. Kroll has her own reality: "It's all gone. Sold up. Theatre closed. Life finished. O Reinhart thank god you never lived to see me old!" This subtle blend of personal and social history is typical of Bond's method.

When Jane Howell directed *Narrow Road to the Deep North*, she felt that it should be played 'like a series of facts. The actors do not get particularly emotionally involved in what they do, they always seek to present the situation to the audience in the clearest and most direct way possible.' That principle is a useful corrective to excessively psychological approaches to acting, and it does underline the need for the performer to work *through* the social facts about the character, and to bring to it a measure of emotional discipline. This is particularly important with episodes of violence, where a very precise effect is aimed for. If, for instance, the Fourth Prisoner, who blinds Lear, does so with any trace of maliciousness or emotional involvement, the point of the scene is lost. The actor must understand the social and political meaning of the blinding. It is done out of expediency, to bring himself to the notice of the authorities, and not because he wants to hurt Lear himself. His motives are determined by the situation, and the actor should not need to invent an emotional motivation divorced from it.

Bond uses an intriguing metaphor to describe a style of acting he feels suits his plays:

> They have to be played with the efficiency of athletes or acrobats. In a lot of modern theatre writing, what is important is the throwing back of the line to each other, like playing tennis, whereas my theatre as far as dialogue is concerned, is like tennis players playing billiards – they have to have that sort of rapport, but they also have to have this plotting and scheming. [14]

The sense of intellectual control this "plotting and scheming" implies, and the rein that it places on emotional indulgence, is especially important for those moments which are emotionally highly-charged, or are in some way expressionistic. Because Bond's plays are so closely-written, it is actually unnecessary for actors or directors to add to the writing in any way. Their job is only to express what is there. It has obviously been of some importance to Bond's career that a director like Bill Gaskill has been responsible for the first productions of most of his work, because he has emphasised meaning, economy and social reality in directing the plays. What can, with the best will in the world, go wrong in production was shown by the Liverpool Everyman's production of *Lear.* In the first scene, soldiers, politicians, Lear and his daughters all burst on to the stage, dressed in day-glo plastics, looking as if they had stepped out of a sports and camping gear shop-window. Bodice and Fontanelle wore, respectively, red and green wiry wigs. The general interpretation was 'correct', inasmuch as there *is* vulgarity in the characters, and the writing *is* condensed and non-naturalistic. However, the vulgarity of the characters has to be understood as the result of a recognisable social reality, not as the expression of bad taste. It therefore needs playing, and staging, in as direct a way as possible. In the same way, the set, which consisted of four scaffolding towers with connecting walkways, making a kind of cage, 'interpreted' the metaphorical cage in which Lear traps himself, and so told the audience what to think about the situation, rather than letting the 'series of facts' do the explaining.

Although Bond can create characters, such as the Queen in *Passion*, or Uncle Sam in *Grandma Faust*, who are part of an agitprop style of cartoon simplicity, most of his work concentrates on the actions of human beings in complex situations, as befits a humanist playwright:

I believe in the mediation of information and experience through the total human-being. I don't believe in reducing characters to their class role or function. That can only confirm audiences in what they already know, or surprise them. Learning is a more subtle experience.

It might seem paradoxical, then, that the kind of performer who serves Bond's style well is often one with experience in variety or comedy, or one who has learnt the essentials of those styles. The casting, in the second production of *Saved,* of Adrienne Posta as Pam, and Queenie Watts as Mary, are good examples, as are Bill Fraser as Lord Radstock in *The Fool* and Roddy Maude-Roxby as the Magician in *Passion*. The comic edge given to even non-comic roles like Pam and Mary, and the very slight hint of the actor's personality that comic acting entails, seems to allow the play to life away from pure emotion so that the audience can assess what it is experiencing. (This is, of course, a very similar notion to Brecht's ideal for the actor, but again, we must be wary of attributing any direct influence from Brecht to Bond.) Some performers become identified with Bond's plays because they bring this lightness of touch and emotional precision to characters who are also tragic. A fine example is Gillian Martell, who has played Georgina in *Narrow Road*, Mrs. Tilehouse in *The Sea*, Judith in *Bingo*, and Mary Lamb in *The Fool*.

The principle of playing facts and situations rather than invented psychologies and emotions is particularly important in the obvious comic scenes of Bond's plays. Comedy, above all, requires that there be some ironic distance between the actor and his performance. When Gaskill directed *Lear* in Munich, he apparently found it difficult to cast actors capable of bringing the necessary dry, ironic humour to those parts played by the English actor Bob Hoskins, a working-class actor with experience in pub and club entertaining. This was particularly important for those parts in which the actor had to perform the beating-up of Warrington or be in charge of the squad that rapes Cordelia. To show how deeply-rooted a sense of the comic is, even in the most unlikely places, we can look again at the blinding of Lear. Here, the Fourth Prisoner's description of the blinding machine as "not an instrument of torture, but a scientific device" is a joke. So too is his description of a straitjacket as a driving coat, and of the headpiece as a crown. They are very serious jokes, told at the expense of the society Lear has helped to create, and although actual laughter will be held in check by what then happens, the audience must nevertheless be offered the humour. The reverse of this is also true. When the comedy is overt, as it is in the rehearsal scene of *The Sea,* it must be held down to its social reality and not be played purely for the effect and the laughs. The rehearsal has to be seen as part of Mrs. Rafi's very serious problem, as well as marvellously comic scene in its own right.

Bond has always been closely associated with first performances of his plays, and has now committed himself to directing all of these himself. His debut as his own director was the National Theatre production of *The Woman* and it brought him into direct contact with the faults and failings of the British acting profession. In a set-up such as that at the National Theatre, the 'versatility' needed to perform *The Woman* on one night and an Ayckbourn play the next proves to be something closer to a kind of prostitution, enforced by the basically exploitative systems under which much of the acting profession labours. Given the unusual scale of the production and the particular demands of the acting, it would be unwise to judge Bond as a director on the basis of *The Woman* alone. What is certain is that the process of directing has suggested to him theoretical links between his playwriting and the actor's craft. Given that the prevailing British acting tradition is emotional/psychological, Bond was inevitably going to conflict with it because his plays require a different approach.

"It's not that I am uninterested in human passions. On the contrary, I think my plays are very passionate plays, but I don't think you can elucidate truth through passion. You can't live history through its psychology. You can't create truth through a psychological apprehension of it. Truth is political, economic, and also personal. But it is not purely personal. There is no truth that you will discover in yourself that you cannot get by watching somebody else in the street. Theatrical truth is a common, shared public truth, and you have to find some way of knowing how to explain that."

Bond's own idea of a narrative theatre, which shows not moments of emotion, but a process in people's lives, implies an approach to understanding experience on the actor's part which he has to share with the writer. That approach is a material one, and is concerned to understand and demonstrate material processes. In his acting notes to *The Woman* Bond writes: "Our acting does not recreate. It recollects. Its energy is intellectual. It makes the particular general and the general particular. It finds the law in the incidental. Thus it restores moral importance to human behaviour."

One of the great reassurances for the actor in a Bond play, and at the same time one of the great challenges, must be the author's craftsmanship of language. His language can be divided into three broad categories, but what really distinguishes Bond is his ability to mix and juxtapose these styles while still maintaining an inner logic. One such style is the 'pared-down naturalism' (Gaskill's phrase) which is, strictly speaking, not naturalistic at all. This is the language of *Saved,* where sentences are short and unrhetorical, in speeches which are also short, and in a specific dialect. It has the surface appearance of one kind of working-class speech, but it is dialogue which distils from its source a powerful dramatic poetry. Bond recognises that there are great strengths in working-class speech, strengths which come from a culture which

is mainly oral rather than literary. "In South London," he told one
interviewer, "they do talk a very virile, and provocative and adequate
language. It can be very terse and epigrammatical; it can be very lyrical, it
can be very passionate and so on." [3]  The second scene of *Saved*, where Pam
and Len sit in the rowing-boat on a bare stage, is full of this kind of poetry.
It is there in the rhythmical patterns of Pam's "Never arst . . . never listen",
or in Len's "I'm 'andy with me 'ands. Yer know, fix up the ol' decoratin'
lark, and knock up a few things." It is there too in the way the two characters
express affection: Pam's "I'm goin' a knit yer a jumper" is a big step towards
Len, even though she hedges her feelings with the qualification "Yer'll 'ave
t'buy the wool." Their language is often touched with a teasing but
fundamentally generous humour:

> LEN: Bin lucky with you. (*His head is in her lap. He twists so that he can
> put his arms round her.*) Ain' I bin lucky with you?

> PAM: Yer don't deserve it.

> LEN: I said I'm sorry – I won't arst no more. It's me good looks done it.

> PAM: It *was* you. It weren't no one else.

> LEN: Less go t'bed early t'night.

> PAM: If yer go t'bed much earlier it won't be worth gettin' up.

The strength of this kind of dialogue is that it is emotionally honest and
accurate, the most precise language for the characters' feelings. It contains
very little rhetoric, and is about the specifics of experience.

It is no accident, then, that some of the most memorable uses of language
occur in the speech of working-class characters, using their natural dialect or
accent. Patty in *The Fool* is a fine example. When Clare complains that his
limbs are on fire. Patty's reply is fierce but witty, and full of powerful
imagery:

> On't talk so daft! Talk straight so a body can have a proper conversation.
> If you're on fire you goo up in smoke. On'y smoke I seen out a you's
> tobacco – when you scrounge it . . . Limbs! Normal people hev arms an'
> legs. Chriss sake talk like a man. On't comfortable with you in the house.
> Talk like some little ol' gal so well bought up she can't git her gloves off
> without the footman. Aches an' pains? I'll know what smartin' is when I
> hev your kid.

Talking of this East Anglian accent Bond says: "I use it because of its
rhythmic vitality, for its curious concrete feel, its repetitions, it's like a sort of
hammer, knocking, knocking, knocking. But at the same time it can be very
agile and very witty. And I use it for its harshness. It's language which imi-
tates experience. By taking that particular dialect you get that solid verbal
feeling in the language. Because language shouldn't be just words. It should
be something that moves in the mouth and forces gestures and action." [14]

When he turns to a more open and expressionistic style of play with *Early
Morning*, a new kind of dialogue appears, a very funny, formal parody of the
speech of the middle and upper classes. It is a style that satirises the moral
evasions made possible by cultivated speech, and the inability to deal with

real experience. At one, splendid, extreme, there is the Queen in *Passion*, who talks like an application form:

> Ideal weather for bowling/swimming/running/jumping/giving a garden party/getting crowned/getting married/making your will/taking in lodgers/lifting up your hearts/counting your blessings/or departing this life. Select the word or phrase of your choice and delete the others as appropriate.

Following the same principle, although closer to naturalism, is the almost Wildean public speech of Mrs. Rafi:

> Get on she says – as if we were drawing water from a tap. I do not know on what level you would find your inspiration – had you been entrusted with a part – but I cannot jump in and out of my part like a lady athlete.

Nevertheless, this style is also capable of expressing Mrs. Rafi's fear of growing old. What it cannot do, which Patty's language can do, is to help her to endure and survive.

The third broad category is the language that some characters use at moments of discovery and learning, a language which is often full of beautiful, formal writing. It is a language of soliloquy, and so it is often honest and direct, but it is also reflective, summing up experience rather than expressing it as it happens. An example, from Scene Three of *Bingo*, is Shakespeare's speech as he sits beneath the gibbetted body of the Young Woman:

> I went to the river yesterday. So quiet. They were all there. No fishing, no boats. One boy to mind the cattle – he was being punished. I watched the fish jump for flies. Then a swan flew by me up the river. On a straight line just over the water. A woman in a white dress running along an empty street. Its neck was rocking like a wave. I heard its breath when it flew by. Sighing. The white swan and the dark water. Straight down the middle of the river and round a curve out of sight. I could still hear its wings. God knows where it was going. So quiet and then silence. (*He stands.*) – noise – dust . . . she saw none of this –

It is dangerous to generalise too widely about a writer's characteristic style, but if anything characterises Bond's, it is a precision and simplicity which can also be very passionate. This can be briefly demonstrated by comparing other translators' versions of Chekhov's *Three Sisters* with Bond's translation. In Elizaveta Fen's version, for instance, Olga tells Irina, 'Your face is positively radiant.' Bond translates this as "Your face is full of light." Ronald Hingley's version has Andrey say in Act Four:

> Where is my past life, oh what has become of it – when I was young, happy and intelligent, when I had such glorious thoughts and visions, and my present and future seemed so bright and promising? Why is it we've hardly started living before we all become dull, drab, boring, lazy, complacent, useless and miserable?

Bond translates this as:

> O where is it? What's happened to my life? I used to be young and happy

Theatre counterpoint: Bodice
knits while Warrington is beaten.
*Lear,* Last Knockings Theatre
Company, Leeds 1972.
(Photo: Tony Coult)

A theatre of action and image:
Scopey's moment of triumph in
*The Pope's Wedding,* Northcott
Theatre, Exeter, 1973.
(Photo: Nicholas Toyne)

and intelligent. I had plans. I still knew how to think. I was confident and the future was full of hope! Why does it happen? – before we've hardly started to live we're already dull, grey, drab, lazy, useless, tired and unhappy?

Although most of Bond's plays contain passages of great literary virtuosity, they are conceived from images and experience, rather than from literary or abstract ideas. *The Sea* for instance, coalesced around two images:

When I was quite young, I was taken to a photographer's shop which over-looked the sea, and I thought that was very curious – the idea of cameras in this room, quite high up, and this sea at the back. And then I heard about somebody who had been drowned after a ship had sunk, and he was found washed up, dead, lying on the beach. And he'd been trying to get his jumper off over his head so that he could swim better – his head was covered by this jumper and his hands were stretched upwards, still caught in the thing, and he'd drowned like that. I just couldn't sit down after I'd heard it. [10]

In a similar way, *Saved* had one of its beginnings in a wartime incident when a flying bomb exploded near him:

There was suddenly this enormous sort of bang which one can't describe, you know, because it's a noise almost inside you. I went along to the park and saw all the trees stripped bare, and picked up this little bird with its head blown off. I would think, very much, that was one of the reasons why I wrote that scene in *Saved*. [10]

The craftsman's commitment to a honing of his skill is evident in the episodes of self-education in theatre such as the two years' intensive playgoing, the work on Chekhov and Brecht, and the preparing of the ground, in the shape of notes, poems, stories, which goes on during the gestation of a play. Some of these find their way eventually into theatre programmes, or form the basis of the prefaces which sometimes accompany the published plays. The conjunction of this very conscious craftsmanship with a fertile imagination results in a genuine theatre poetry, which is an event in time and space, as well as literary artefact.

If the Royal Court Writers' Group helped lay the foundations for the principle of a "theatre of action and images", Bond's instinct for arresting and disturbing imagery rooted in physical reality is something far more personal. What distinguishes it from the more meretricious use of theatre effect is the precision of the stage images in relation to the themes of the the play. For example, the cricket match in *The Pope's Wedding* shows the audience Scopey's moment of triumph, important for us to see because his later move into fantasy has to be perceived as a decline from a position of strength. The actual sight of Scopey's triumph also lends him the sexual dignity which makes Pat's lines after they have made love – "You look beautiful all in white . . . Sounds like a bride" – more than just a vague fantasy or metaphor. Our having seen Scopey ecstatically hitting cricket balls about the field, and shouting, several times over "Yes! Yes! Yes!" makes her lines, and her feelings seem fully justified. On another level, in *The Sea*, Hatch's frenzied cutting of yards of curtaining material seems almost like an act of violence. Bond plays on our reaction to the 'wasteful' cutting-up of yards of furnishing material, but he links that reaction to Hatch's crushed spirit which has been caused by precisely that ethos, of small business and even smaller respect for human potential, that makes us worry about seeing the velvet slashed and torn.

A play's opening scene is usually a good guide to the writer's skill, and the opening scene of *Lear*, for example, shows with what economy and speed character, location and society are conveyed. On the empty stage sits a stack of building materials. Suddenly, on to the stage erupt first three workmen carrying a body, then a soldier. There is panic because someone is coming who mustn't see the body. One of the men shouts: "Go back, go back! Work!", and a tarpaulin is flung over the body.

The presence of a soldier, the lack of respect accorded to the body, the panicky instructions, and the obvious atmosphere of fear all suggest an unjust, dangerous kind of society. All this establishing information is conveyed in just one page of the published script, and almost entirely in physical action. When Lear enters to inspect the site, he discovers the body, accuses one of the workers of causing the death, and institutes a drumhead trial for sabotage (but not, significantly, for murder). The extraordinary speed of events demonstrates Lear's absolute power and the whole atmosphere of repression and legitimised violence that he trails in his wake. The formality of the scene (Bill Gaskill described it in rehearsal as like a Royal Visit to a shipyard) allows the King to make general statements of policy, and the conflict these cause with his daughters establishes their characters. The rest of the scene shows power sliding from one centre, Lear, to another, his daughters. Again, the shift is accomplished with great speed, but also with wit and panache. From Bodice's protest, "Father, if you kill this man, it will be an injustice", through to the daughters' departure to prepare a council of war, Bond sets up a series of moral expectations only to show them abandoned moments later. The picture we get is of a society where values are fluid and expedient, where the relationship between father and daughter is corrupted, where a man may be summarily executed on negligible evidence. All this, most of it demonstrated in action, gives the audience all the information necessary to understand the play.

One of Bond's most characteristic pieces of stagecraft is a kind of theatre counterpoint, where two events are juxtaposed, sometimes in ironic contrast, sometimes to enlarge and explain the individual actions. With this technique, actions are always held in some kind of qualifying frame. Events are thus seen as happening relative to other events, and not as self-sufficient, inevitable incidents. A clear example of this is the park scene in *The Fool*. Here the society world of Mrs. Emmerson, Lord Radstock, and the Lambs is pitted against a brutal fist-fight in which an Irishman and a black man beat each other up so that sporting gentlemen can bet on them. Upstage, the fight goes on, and downstairs there is talk of poetry. The total stage-picture shows that the fight for money is a necessary precondition for the polite discussion of poetry. It is an ironic contrast in which two opposing tendencies exist together on the stage just as they do in the value-system of the society being portrayed.

In the park scene of *The Fool*, the contrast is quite explicit, and the commentary direct. More oblique, and sometimes far more disturbing, can be Bond's technique of counterpointing emotion. A remarkable example of this is the beating-up of Warrington in *Lear*, in which a nauseating and horrific torturing of Lear's old minister occurs within a framework of class comedy. Soldier A, to whom the techniques of torture are professional skills, as familiar as stripping a rifle or blancoing webbing, discusses matters with Bodice: "Yer wan 'im done in a fancy way? Thass sometimes arst for. I once 'ad t'cut a throat for some ladies t'see once . . . I once give a 'and t'flay a man. I couldn't manage that on me own . . ." As the soldier sets about kicking and punching Warrington, Bodice settles herself onto her riding stick and begins to knit. Fontanelle, meanwhile, leaps around the torturer and his victim like a demented schoolgirl: "Do something! Don't let him get away with it. O Christ, why did I cut his tongue out? I want to hear him scream." Bodice knits on, apparently unconcerned, save for a dismissive aside to the audience about her sister's behaviour. Then she asks the soldier to play-act begging for Warrington's life, so that she can play-act refusing his pardon. After that, she 'playfully' deafens Warrington with her knitting needles. Both sisters are obviously mad, and their behaviour is grimly comic. But all the time, Warrington is being mutilated near to death. To describe the scene so baldly might make it seem inexcusably cynical and tasteless. In performance the opposite effect is achieved, and Bond's technique of emotional counter-point creates a riveting tension in which comedy frames and controls the violence. The actual act of violence provokes a strong emotion of reaction, as it should do. Left to speak for itself, it would provoke only disgust, despair, or an impotent desire for revenge. With the comedy to control it, and comedy which itself makes points about the peculiar class-relationship between the soldier and the two sisters, the audience's judgement is solicited, so holding the emotion in check without for a moment diminishing it. The result is a heightened sense of outrage, tinged with understanding – a very complex and rewarding effect for a playwright to achieve.

The technique is taken still further in the lynching scene of *The Swing*. Again, there is a comic frame, in the parody of American law-and-order rhetoric from Skinner, and there is also the further ironic framework of the theatre building itself, and the performance elements in it. Inside these frames, the legal murder takes place, and there is added irony in the real audience's having to act as the audience within the play. So while we are caught up in the dreadful events on stage, we are at the same time distanced and made critically aware of the factors that have brought these events into being.


Bond's treatment of violent action has often been misrepresented as cathartic, or confused with irrelevant notions such as Artaud's Theatre of Cruelty. What seems to happen is that critics respond to actions such as the stoning in *Saved* as isolated, real events, not theatre events in a theatre structure which gives them a valid context. Events, especially violent ones, in Bond's work have both causes and consequences, and cannot be seen in isolation. Sometimes the context may seem, of itself, insignificant. Thus, the stoning of the baby in *Saved* is so surprising because it takes place in a park. As Gaskill wrote in the programme notes to the first production: 'I think what Edward Bond shows in the play is not only the violence but also the ordinariness at the same time . . . he has to demonstrate both the truth of the violence and the truth of the apathy . . .'

By dwelling on acts of violence there is a risk of playing into the hands of those who see his work only in these terms. However, it is worth considering why violence does shock so much in performance. The answer lies partly in the sensuality of Bond's imagery. He is able to evoke the vulnerability and the dignity of the human body with a painter's skill. (There are images, such as that of the gibbetted girl in *Bingo*, and the autopsy in *Lear* which trace their origins to Rembrandt, and there are other scenes that suggest Blake, such as the two daughters visiting Lear in prison.) *The Swing* contrasts two scenes in which the vulnerability and the dignity of the human body are at the heart of the action. The first incident is Greta's baring of her breast. Bond shows that, for once, her actions almost transcend the normal game-playing of sexual tactics condoned by society. Her words are significant: "How firm the nipple is. It glows. It means I like you, Ralph. When the lady's breasts are firm, it means she likes the man. Always remember. The sign of fondness." The stage direction "*gently*", the physical detail of her body, the use of the words "glows", "like", "fondness" all strengthen the sense that Greta has, for this one moment, found an equilibrium. Her emotional and her physical lives blend together. But very soon after, guilt and fear take over and the two lives slip out of synchronisation so rapidly that she goes mad. Because of that madness, induced in her because her society lives in a permanent state of polite sexual hysteria, the shooting of Fred becomes inevitable. The shooting seems doubly offensive because it comes after a moment of near-sanity. The dignity of the body is established, and then desecrated. It is worth remembering that Paul, at the beginning of the play, tells the audience that "he died very easy compared t'the style of some lynchin's" and that what we see is only a man being shot dead, which has been, after all, one of the staple ingredients of art and entertainment since guns were invented. What Bond does here is to re-awaken the audience's sensitivity. The stage direction that Fred is "*white with terror*", his tying to a flower-decked swing, and his pleading all emphasise the victim's complete vulnerability. When the shooting actually starts, the stage directions are very precise and orchestrated: "*Fred jerks violently. Screams . . . spins, twists, jerks, screams. Blood spurts. Lights snap out for a second, flash, come back to half, snap up to full.*" Skinner runs to the swing to push it, and runs back "*shaking blood from his hands*". Finally, Fred "*swings slowly and silently upside-down. Blood drips and swishes over the stage*". Anything less precise than those directions, and less detailed than the social context shown, and the shooting would become mere thrill-mongering. Because Bond insists on the audience knowing what happens when bullets hit a body, and shows the audience the absurdity of events that cause that to happen, the shooting generates overwhelming emotion, and, at the same time, compassionate understanding.

Bond has a very strong visual sense, and some of the most important events in his plays are stage-pictures in which the arrangement of people and sets and props on the stage is as potent as anything that the characters are saying. The obvious example is Len's chair-mending at the end of *Saved*, but as remarkable is the clifftop scene from *The Sea*, with its upright piano, town banner, and bowed figures, or that extraordinary stage direction in *The Fool*: *"Milton opens the door in the windows and goes out. He disappears. The door swings slowly open. It catches the sun. It flashes once in the room. Brilliantly. Silence. An owl calls in the trees."* Bond has always defined his sets very closely so that they support the human action that they contain, but do not dominate it (except in cases like Lear's Wall where the domination is part of the play's action). This is how he defines his attitude towards sets:

> I think that a lot of scenery detracts or creates an illusion. I want to stress, increase, a sense of reality in the theatre. When something dramatic, moving or profound happens to people outside the theatre, we concentrate (usually) on those people because they are our real interest . . . Also a lot of beautiful scenery can become parasitic on the action – and of course, designers themselves recognise this. A further practical point is that as my plays have short scenes, and the contrasts between the locations of these scenes is often important, there would be no time to set up too elaborate scenery.

It would be possible to plunder the history of literature, theatre and art finding echoes, influences and quotations in Edward Bond's plays. He is almost unfashionably widely-read, a happy result perhaps of having had no formal education at all. Certain names though, such as Shakespeare, Chekhov and Blake, are unavoidable. It is Brecht's name, however, that occurs most frequently in discussion about Bond. It is true, of course, that Bond has not been directly influenced by Brecht, except in the sense that there was a generalised Brechtian influence in the air, affecting directors as much as writers, at the time Bond was making contact with the Royal Court. He is however, a Brecht-like writer in many ways. In a television programme about Brecht, Bond explained: "The good thing about Brecht was that he was a liberator, in the sense that he restored to writers the whole world. You didn't have to write about little things any more. The important things could be written about."

However, no amount of comparison or analysis can actually capture the experience of good theatre, and nothing can substitute for performance. The theatre alone of all the art forms gives access to the most important and subtle and constructive ideas, because it is the medium that is at once most immediate and personal, and yet most social. As Bond himself explains it:

> I think perhaps one should write very simple plays – with a direct message – and also more complex plays that are an analysis, an investigation, a testing. The stage seems an ideal place to do both these things. Firstly it can have great panache and wit. And, for the more complex work, you have a combination of things that the other arts can only use selectively. The human face is like a mobile canvas constantly re-arranging the image, the figure is like a mobile sculpture, but it can be statuesque. Speech is a form of music, conveying much of what it says through tone and rhythm. So communication in theatre is very complex and subtle and intimate.

This short book necessarily fails to evoke the full richness of Bond's "complex and subtle and intimate" work, ideally achieved best in performance. I have tried to make some sorely needed basic statements about it, by suggesting some of the ways in which the plays work both in the theatre, and in the minds and emotions of audiences and readers. In the end, what is vitally important about Bond's work is its dogged and insistent glorying in humanity and its possibilities. Inseparable from that quality of vision is a remarkable technical and artistic skill. Together, the two qualities offer indispensable visions for our dangerous and despairing times.

# BIBLIOGRAPHY

The quotations by Edward Bond used in this book are taken from interviews with, and journalism by, him, and also from private correspondence. A full bibliography of the publicly available interviews and journalism is contained in *Edward Bond: A Companion to the Plays,* published by TQ Publications, 44 Earlham Street, London WC2 and compiled by Malcolm Hay and Philip Roberts, who are working on a full-length study to be called *The Theatre of Edward Bond,* due to be published by Eyre Methuen in 1980. The following is a selective list of the sources I have found most useful:

## a. Interviews and Assessments

| | | |
|---|---|---|
| 1 *Plays and Players* | Nov. 1965 | Interview by Robert Cushman |
| 2 *The Guardian* | 11.4.66 | Interview by Derek Malcolm |
| 3 *Transatlantic Review* | Autumn 1966 | Interview by Giles Gordon |
| 4 *Sunday Times* | 31.3.68 | Interview by Alen Brien |
| 5 *Observer* | 9.2.69 | Interview by Ronald Bryden |
| 6 *Peace News* | 10.4.69 | Interview by Arthur Arnold |
| 7 *Gambit* | vol.5, no.17, 1970 | Interview by John Calder, Irving Wardle, Harold Hobson, Jane Howell |
| 8 *The Guardian* | 29.9.71 | Interview by John Hall |
| 9 *New York Times* | 21.1.72 | Assessment by Charles Marowitz |
| 10 *Theatre Quarterly* | vol.II, no.5, Jan-Mar 1972 | Interview by the Editors |
| 11 *Revolutions in Modern Drama* | G. Ballard & Sons, London 1972 | Final chapter is an assessment of Bond by Katherine J. Worth |
| 12 *The Times* | 22.5.73 | Interview by Ronald Hayman |
| 13 *The Guardian* | 14.8.73 | Interview by Hugh Hebert |
| 14 *Plays and Players* | Dec. 1975 | Interview by Tony Coult |
| 15 *New Society* | 11.12.75 | Assessment by Albert Hunt |
| 16 *Writers and their Work: Edward Bond* | Longmans for the British Council, 1976 | Assessment by Simon Trussler |
| 17 *Performing Arts Journal* | vol.1, no.2, Fall 1976 | Interview by Glen Loney |
| 18 *Observer Magazine* | 18.7.76 | Interview by John Walker |
| 19 *The Guardian* | 24.11.76 | Interview by Nicholas de Jongh |
| 20 *Theatre Quarterly* | vol.VII, no.28 | Interview by the Editors |

| | | |
|---|---|---|
| 21 *Time Out* | No.406 | Interview by Tony Coult |
| 22 *Observer* | 15.1.78 | Interview by Victoria Radin |
| 23 *Observer Magazine* | 6.8.78 | Interview by Malcolm Hay and Philip Roberts |
| 24 *Time Out* | No.436 | Interview by Cathy Itzin |
| 25 *Theatre Quarterly* | Vol.VIII No.30 | 'Brecht, Bond, Gaskill and Political Theatre |
| 26. *Arts North* | March/April 1979 | Interview |
| 27. *Canadian Theatre Review* | Fall 1979 | Interview, re 'The Woman', by Tony Coult |

## b. Journalism

| | | |
|---|---|---|
| 28 *The Guardian* | 13.1.66 | 'The Greatest Hack' (about Thomas Middleton) |
| 29 *Censorship* | Autumn 1966 | 'Censor in Mind' (about the censoring of *Saved*) |
| 30 *The Critic* | 1.3.68 | 'Critics Reviewed' (about theatre criticism) |
| 31 *The Sunday Times* | 25.11.73 | 'Beating Barbarism' (reply to points made by Harold Hobson in his review of *Bingo*) |
| 32 *The Guardian* | 14.1.78 | 'Work in Hand' (about the responsibilities of the writer) |
| 33 *Plays and Players* | October 1978 | "Us, Our Drama, and the National Theatre" (on the occasion of NT production of "The Woman") |

## c. Poems

| | | |
|---|---|---|
| *Theatre Poems and Songs* | Eyre Methuen, 1978 | A selection of poems written on, for and around the plays. |

## d. Programme Notes

The Summer 1975 issue of *Fireweed* magazine contains a shortened version of Bond's introduction to his translation of *Spring Awakening*, under the title *The Murder of Children*.

'In Defence of Shakespeare' – Programme note for R.S.C. Small-Scale Tour of Much Ado about Nothing and The Caucasian Chalk Circle, 1979.

### e. Production Casebooks

| *Theatre Quarterly* | vol.II, no.5, Jan-Mar 1975 | Casebook on *Lear* at the Royal Court |
| *Theatre Quarterly* | vol.VI, no.21 | Casebook on *The Fool* at the Royal Court (plus interview with the director, Peter Gill) |

### f. Plays

*Saved*, Methuen London 1966; second ed., 1969; Hill & Wang, New York 1966

*Early Morning*, Calder and Boyars, London 1968

*Narrow Road to the Deep North*, Methuen, London 1968; Hill & Wang, New York 1969

*The Pope's Wedding*, Methuen, London 1971 (also includes the short stories, *Mr Dog* and *The King with Golden Eyes*, and *Sharpeville Sequence* – 'Poem: I Cannot Mourn', 'Scene: Black Mass', 'Poem: Bird', 'Story: Christ Wanders and Waits', 'Poem: Rest')

*Lear*, Eyre Methuen, London 1972; Hill & Wang, New York 1972

*The Sea*, Eyre Methuen, London 1973; Hill & Wang, New York 1975 (in a volume with *Bingo*)

*Bingo*, Eyre Methuen, London 1974 (also includes *Passion*); Hill & Wang, New York 1975 (in a volume with *The Sea*)

*The Fool* and *We Come to the River*, Eyre Methuen, London 1976

*A-A-America!* and *Stone*, Eyre Methuen, London 1976

*The Bundle*, Eyre Methuen, London 1978

*The Woman*, Eyre Methuen, London 1979; Hill & Wang, New York 1979

*Plays: One*, Eyre Methuen, London 1977 (contains *The Pope's Wedding*, *Saved* and a substantially revised version of *Early Morning*)

*Plays: Two*, Eyre Methuen, London 1978 (contains *Narrow Road to the Deep North, Lear, The Sea, Black Mass* and *Passion*)

Any play referred to in the text that is not published or about to be published is not available. Edward Bond would like it to be made clear that he will not make these scripts available, publicly or privately.

**Index to Bond's works mentioned in the text**